I0359743

The No-B.S.* Rules for Taking Care of Your Money
*NO BORING STUFF

How to Keep More of What You Earn
and Build a Strong Financial Foundation

One Consumer

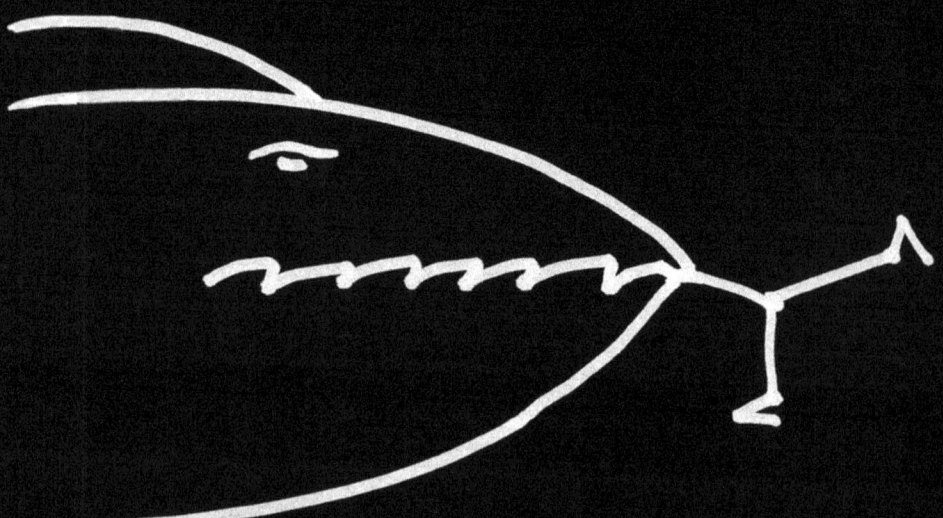

Two Consumers

Why You Should Read This Book

This book has been written for people who are interested in money and who don't want to deal with a lot of B.S.—Boring Stuff.

If you're just getting started, if you are digging out of a hole, or if you just want to simplify your life—this book is for you.

Money. Pretty much everyone has some money. For most of us, it's the reward for doing some kind of work.

And as soon as we get money—we are under pressure to spend it. Food. Shelter. Clothing. And more. In the United States—much, much more. Everybody wants your money.

We live in what experts say is a "consumer economy." More than 70 percent of the economic activity in this country is a result of people spending the money they earn—maybe spending even more than the money they earn.

Encouraging that spending? That's a job for advertising and marketing. Anyone with any money to spend becomes a target. In today's data-driven environment, marketers go after their prey with ruthless, clinical efficiency.

To help support our consumer economy, the United States has developed a vast, lucrative financial services industry. Banking. Loans. Insurance. Investing. Credit reporting. And services—lots and lots of services. The finance industry is deeply involved in nearly every aspect of American life. Its success depends, in large measure, on making our financial lives complicated.

The Rules in this book are focused on keeping things simple, avoiding debt and living life free and clear. Think of it as financial serenity. *The Rules* are conservative. They don't encourage taking big risks. They urge restraint and, at times, sacrifice. But if you want to be able to relax and stop worrying about money, sometimes that's what you have to do.

This book takes a skeptical view of a lot of the things that are commonly taken for granted. Just because "everybody" does something doesn't mean it's necessarily a good idea. Car loans, for example—bad deal. Don't do them. Car leases? Even worse. And student loans? This book goes into detail about the student loan trap.

What it all gets down to is this: You work hard for your money. Don't you deserve to keep some of it?

You may not agree with everything you read here, but it will encourage you to think things through. When you are making a financial decision, you'll be able to think about it in terms of *The Rules*. Which rules apply? What do they suggest? How will that affect your thinking? What will you decide?

Read this book so you can be confident you understand a sound set of basic principles you can use to guide your personal financial decision making.

Other Works by this Author

The Incompleat Sound Operator
The Richest Man in New Babylon
Murder & Miss Austen's Ball
MuchAdoAboutNothingDotCom
 A Play with Rhymes
 for Modern Times

The No-B.S.* Rules for Taking Care of Your Money
*NO BORING STUFF

How to Keep More of What You Earn
and Build a Strong Financial Foundation

RIDGE KENNEDY
Author of *The Richest Man in New Babylon*

A Publication of the
Financial Wisdom Foundation

HEDGEHOG HOUSE

West Orange, New Jersey 07052

Tel: 973-400-9738
www.hedgehoghousebooks.com

ISBN Paper: 978-1-951989-32-3
E-Book: 978-1-951989-33-0

Publisher's Cataloging-in-Publication Data
Names: Kennedy, Ridgway, author. Kennedy, Ridge, author
Title: The No B.S. Rules for Taking Care of Your Money / Ridgway Kennedy, Ridge Kennedy
Description: First Edition. West Orange, New Jersey
Hedgehog House Books
Identifiers: LCCN: 2022902554 | ISBN 978-1-951989-32-3
1. Personal Finance 2. Debt
Library of Congress Control Number: 2022902554
Cover Design by Barnett-Dubé

Editor: Pam Eidson
E before i Document Editing
www.ebeforei.xyz ebeforei.xyz@gmail.com

Typesetting by Affinity Publisher

Copyright © 2025 by S. Ridgway Kennedy

All rights reserved. No part of this publication may be reproduced, distributed, or transmitted in any form or by any means, including photocopying, recording, or other electronic or mechanical methods, without the prior written permission of the publisher, except in the case of brief quotations embodied in critical reviews and certain other noncommercial uses permitted by copyright law. For permission requests, write to the publisher, addressed "Attention: Permissions Coordinator," at the address above or permissions@hedgehoghousebooks.com.

10 9 8 7 6 5 4 3 2 1

Dedication

To Jane,
who makes everything I do possible

The Richest Man Project

CAUTION: The following text is borderline Boring Stuff.
Feel free to skip the rest of this page.

Dear Reader,

In 2020, I wrote *The Richest Man in New Babylon*. Its publication was the culmination of more than 13 years of work, maybe longer if you include the entire time I worked at the New Jersey Society of Certified Public Accountants.

I wasn't an accountant, merely a writer and public relations guy. But, in my role as a writer/PR guy, I spent a lot of time speaking with financial professionals and writing stories about personal financial planning. I interviewed experts and wrote about their recommendations for taking care of money.

Several personal financial planning specialists pointed me toward a book titled *The Richest Man in Babylon*. That volume by George S. Clason is a collection of pamphlets written during the 1920s in a simulated ancient dialect and set in Babylon circa 5000 BCE. These experts remembered Clason's work not so much because it was deeply researched or well written. They remembered it because of its simplicity. It offered its readers a set of common sense "laws" based on timeless wisdom.

In my book, *The Richest Man in New Babylon*, I extracted the fundamental truths from Clason's pamphlets and augmented them with the principles used by modern certified personal financial planners. They became *"The Rules."*

I created a story set in a modern American city. A young man faces huge financial challenges, but he gets lucky. He meets a man who promises to introduce him to the richest man in the city, someone who might be willing to share the secrets of how to attain great wealth.

It's a good book and a good story for some audiences. But it is male-centered and . . . it is a story. Many people today don't have the patience to read a story. Just the facts—that's what they want.

So I wrote this book. Just the facts. Just *The Rules*. Just the stuff you really ought to know. No B.S.

No. Boring. Stuff.

Ridge

Contents

Part I
Elements & Properties

Elements & Properties 4

The Periodic Table
of financial Elements 5

Debt 8

Part II
The No B.S* Rules

Big Picture: The U.S. Economy 12

Rule No. 1 16

Rule No. 2 22

Rule No. 3 28

Rule No. 4 36

Seven Steps for Getting
Out of Debt 40

Rule No. 5 44

Rule No. 6 48

Rule No. 7 52

Rule No. 8 58

Rule No. 9 64

Rule No. 10 72

And in Conclusion 74

Part III:
The Appendices

Appendix A
The Emergency
Savings Fund Crisis 79

Appendix B
Earning Interest Ain't Easy 80

Appendix C
How to Check & Correct
Your Credit Report 83

Appendix D
Dealing with Debt Collectors 88

Part III:
The Appendices (continued)

Appendix E
Education and Avoiding
the Student Loan Trap 89

Appendix F
Life Is Better
without a Car Loan 97

Appendix G
Investment Advice
from a Rich Man 101

Appendix H
The Affordable Housing Crisis 102

Appendix I
Cryptocurrency and NFTs 105

Appendix J
Savings and Retirement 107

Appendix K
Credit Unions versus Banks 110

Appendix L
Can You Trust
the Stock Market? 111

Part IV
Glossary

Glossary 117

Part V
Parting Shots

A Letter from an Old Man 139

How to Get the Most
Out of This Book 141

Get Involved 144

Stone Soup—A Recipe 145

Resources 148

Acknowledgments 153

About the Author 155

Guarantee and Warning

The No B.S.* Guarantee

The following pages have been carefully reviewed, inspected, and are guaranteed to be 100 percent free of Boring Stuff (B.S).

No B.S. was used in the initial preparation of the text. All research passed through a micron-level B.S. filtration system. The writing process was conducted in a B.S.-free environment to prevent cross-contamination.

If, upon review, a reader detects B.S., a warranty claim may be filed with the publisher. Please submit claims by email to the publisher (publisher@hedgehoghousebooks.com), identifying the offending B.S. by page and paragraph. Photocopies of pages with passages highlighted will be accepted. All warranty claims will be taken under close advisement and, if the offending material is determined to be, in fact, B.S., it will be edited to make it un-boring. If the cited content is determined to be pure, unadulterated, and uncorrectable B.S., it will be deleted from all future editions of this book and the claim filer will be gratefully acknowledged.

Experts in economics and representatives of commercial business interests may consider the contents of this book, in the whole or in part, **radical and subversive**. Strict adherence to the principles of personal financial management as described here may—in addition to **helping you keep more of your money for your own use**—cause a **recession** in the automotive industry, **result in the failure** of certain educational enterprises, and **disrupt the economy of the United States of America. Use the content of this book with great care.**

Editor's Note: We believe the author was, in the text contained in the warning above, engaging some kind of exaggeration for emphasis or possibly a humorous effect. We argued strenuously that it ought to be deleted because readers might believe it and be worried, but to no avail. We can assure readers, however, based on extensive research, that their application of *The Rules* supplied herein will result in nothing more serious than the attainment of greater control of their personal finances and retention of more of the money they earn.

How to Use This Book
A summary of the parts of this book and the best way to use them.

Part I: Elements & Properties
Read this. It's short. It's theory. It explains where *The Rules* come from.

Part II: The Rules
Okay, this is why you've got this book. **Pay attention!**

First, read this section of the book. Get your head around *The Rules*. Next, reread *The Rules*. Be sure you understand *The Rules*. Then figure out how you're going to keep score.

Now comes the most important part: Follow *The Rules*.

Keep score. Don't do dumb things. Follow *The Rules*. Don't quit on yourself. Yes, you can do this.

Follow *The Rules*. Keep score. Don't quit. And remember: Success is all up to you. It's your responsibility! **But** you *do not* have to do it alone.

Part III: The Appendices
A few important topics require extra attention. This information may, however, only apply to a limited number of people and therefore seem like Boring Stuff to some readers. The expanded material is in the appendices. The subjects include student loan debt, credit reports, credit scores, basic investment strategies, and similar topics. If any of them apply to you and your situation, you will find information you can use.

Part IV: The Glossary
This is not a textbook. No Boring Stuff, right? But you need a good understanding of the words, terms, and jargon associated with money and personal finance. Why? Because it's terminology (lingo) that HR managers, bankers, and financial product sales reps are going to throw at you.

A Glossary subheading at the end of the description of each rule is followed by a list of words, acronyms, and phrases. **This is terminology that you need to know and understand**. If you see an entry on one of these lists and you do not immediately know what it means with respect to you and your money, *you need to find out!* These terms are defined in the *Glossary* section. **Study each unfamiliar glossary entry and its definition**. And, boring as it may be, it would be a **good idea to read the whole darn Glossary**.

Part V: Parting Shots
End of the line. A note from the author. Recommendations on how to use this book. Additional resources, acknowledgments, and even a recipe.

Part I
Elements & Properties

Everything You Need to Know in Order to Understand Personal Financial Management

Elements & Properties

Element

el·e·ment

/ˈelǝmǝnt/

noun

1. a key essential piece of a complex construction.
2. an essential fundamental of a branch of knowledge.
3. each of more than one hundred substances that cannot be broken down into simpler substances; the primary constituents of matter.

Property

pro-per-ty

/ˈpräpǝrdē/

noun

1. an attribute, quality, or characteristic of something.
2. a thing or things belonging to someone; possessions.

The Periodic Table of Financial Elements

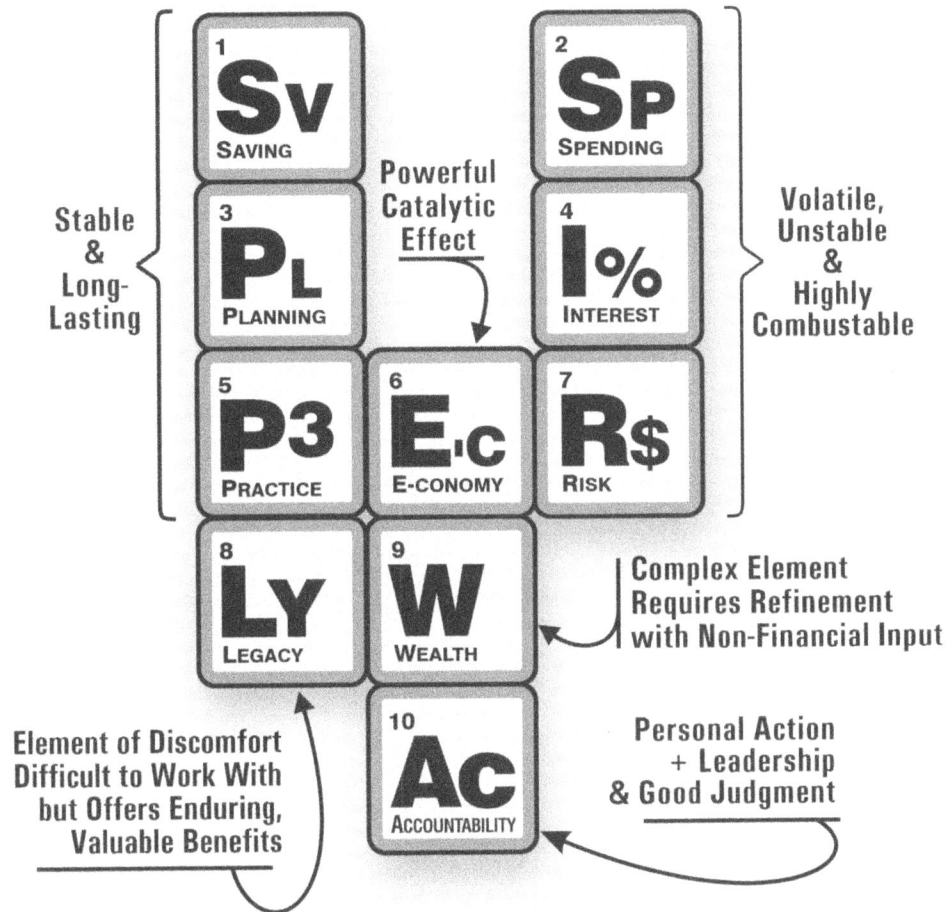

The Elements & Their Properties

Saving
The most powerful element. Provides strength. Facilitates decisions. Assures achievement. Enables financial security.

Spending
The most active element. Easily excited by external stimuli. Combines easily with other elements, frequently resulting in excessive amounts of "stuff" and waste.

Planning
Invaluable time-based element. Allows users to begin new endeavors successfully. Equally useful in breaking down large challenges and achieving major goals.

Interest
The most volatile element. Offers modest beneficial effects when applied in some financial situations. Unfortunately, it may have powerful, corrosive, highly destructive effects in others.

Practice
Active element in two states. In its solid state, represents proficiency and professionalism, valued skills, recognition, and income. In its fluid state, it provides repeated exercise for growth and improved proficiency.

The Building Blocks of Personal Finance

E-conomy
A newly discovered element. First detected in silicon chips this element, once rare, permeates every aspect of personal finance today. Understanding how to use this element with its related apps and devices is essential.

Risk
The element of uncertainty. Present in economic systems designed to multiply a financial stake, as well as in schemes designed to protect against financial adversity.

Legacy
The element of absolute certainty. Found, most critically, in the inescapable human states of dying and death. Also significantly present in conditions such as memory, reputation, and philanthropy.

Wealth
An element easily confused with money. A complex, high order element that encompasses measurable and unmeasurable rewards and aspects of life. May include a powerful spiritual dimension.

Accountability
The element of personal responsibility, calling individuals to account for action. Also present in the relationships formed between individuals including life partners, close friends, and trusted advisors.

What about Debt?

Pay attention! *Understand this clearly!* **DEBT IS NOT AN ELEMENT!** It is *NOT* an essential component of personal financial management.

Debt is a caustic compound created when Sp (Spending) is greater than Sv (Saving).

Debt is a burden. Debt is overhead. **Debt produces harmful, wasteful side effects—side effects such as MORE DEBT!**

Debt is NOT normal!

Financial service companies and any business that sells just about anything *want you to think debt is normal!*

Why?

Why do *you* think businesses want you to think that debt is normal?

*Why do they want you to think **everybody** should be in debt?*

Why?

Because they all want to sell you more stuff.

Because they all want you to buy their services and products.

Because they want your money!

Organizations that promote the official, mainstream brand of financial education (a.k.a. "Financial Literacy") encourage students to learn about "managing debt." They want students to learn how to "get the best deal" on a car loan. They think people need to know how to shop for the "best interest rates" for credit cards.

BORING STUFF!

Here's what you really need to know.

AVOID DEBT!

Read on. We'll help you do that.

The Rules

Rule

rule

/ˈrül/

noun

1. an approved procedure for conduct or action.
2. a statement about things that are or should be done and what is not allowed to be done.
3. a piece of advice about the best way to do something.

verb

1. exercise power, authority, or influence over something.

Turning Elements & Properties into *The Rules*

Elements and properties represent a theoretical approach to a subject; a useful way to think about things. Theory is helpful when you are trying to understand, analyze, and discuss a topic. Theory is less useful when it comes to taking action.

Question: *How do we turn theory into practice?*

Answer: *Create rules.*

Boil the theory down according to the properties, and condense it into clear statements that can be used to guide action. Step by step. One element at a time.

Part II

The No B.S.* Rules

*No Boring Stuff

Big Picture: The U.S. Economy

If you want to survive and thrive financially in the United States, there is one very important thing you need to understand and always keep in mind.

The System Is Rigged.

According to government statistics, the richest 1 percent of Americans possess 10 times as much wealth as the bottom 50 percent of the U.S. population. By every measure, rich people get richer and poor people stay poor. People in the middle lose ground.

Wealthy people *and the businesses they own or invest in* can spend unlimited amounts of money in their efforts to influence state and federal legislators and agencies. As a result, they block regulations they don't like, write laws they do like, and create even bigger financial *and political* advantages for themselves.

By any standard, the U.S. has the highest overall healthcare costs in the world. It also has a higher rate of chronic illness and a lower overall life expectancy than more than 20 other high-income nations. The U.S. does not provide universal health insurance coverage. Approximately one American out of every seven does not have any health insurance.

The cost of housing—rentals and purchases—has doubled, in inflation-adjusted dollars, since 1970. Average incomes in the U.S. have remained relatively unchanged. More than half a million people in the U.S. are homeless.

The average American will pay about $280,000—**more than a quarter of a million dollars**—in interest during their lifetime.

One of the simplest ways people can take control of their financial lives is by saving—putting money in a savings account. Unfortunately, the interest rates for savings are generally lower than the rate of inflation. In recent years, interest on savings has been less than 1 percent. **The American financial system does not reward people for saving.**

So What are We Going to Do?

The U.S. brand of capitalism, with inequality and a degree of unfairness built into it, is the world we live it. It kinda sucks. It is definitely not perfect. But it's better than a lot of other places in the world.

Despite the advantages that wealthy people possess, **there is room for the rest of us to improve our situation as individuals.**

Sure, we can try to make things better for everyone (see *Fixing the Wealth Inequality* box below), but that isn't going to happen quickly. So, as individuals and families, we have to find the best strategy for surviving and thriving—attaining financial security—in the U.S. economy as it currently exists.

Everyone in this so-called consumer economy—***everyone***—wants your money!

The American economy is built on marketing, borrowing, and selling us a lot of stuff that we don't need. Furthermore, we pay extra transaction fees, interest, taxes, and other costs. Looking toward the future, we find countless investment options with little or no guarantee for returns.

Managing your money in America is complicated. Confusing. Full of pitfalls and fine print.

Why is that?

It's because the people who want to take your money like it that way. If we are confused, it makes it easier for them.

So, let's simplify things. Fight back against the system in our own small way. Get rid of the complicated Boring Stuff (B.S.) and make things clear.

Follow *The Rules!*

Most of *The Rules* are as old as the clay tablets of ancient Mesopotamia. But there are some new ones to help us address timeless matters by working with modern tools.

The Rules help you know what to do. **They help you cut through the B.S. and focus on what's important.** Any time you face a financial challenge or dilemma, you can break it down. Which rules apply? What does that mean for you? Work it out. **Then follow *The Rules*.**

Do you want to have more money?

Follow *The Rules!*

NOTE: Fixing the Wealth Inequality/Unfairness Problems in the U.S.

If you agree that the system is rigged, and that it's a problem, join organizations that address the problem. Inform yourself. Join a union. Most of all, if you are eligible, be sure you are registered to vote. Then vote! Encourage your friends to get involved, too. Network. Communicate. Make voting your number one civic priority.

Rule No. 1

Pay Yourself First.

Rule No. 1: Pay Yourself First.

You've got some money. You've got a job. Maybe it's a great job. Maybe it's a terrible job and you want to move on. But you work hard and you earn every penny you get. Or maybe you get disability or Social Security. Somehow, some way, you've got money coming in.

Don't you deserve to be able to keep some of it?

Here's how money works for most people. Maybe not you, but for most people.

1. You get some money. You tell yourself that you will pay your bills and, *if there is any money left over*, you will save some of it.

2. You pay your most important bills such as rent, food, and utilities. And there are always more bills, even some you can't pay.

3. There's no money left over and **you are BROKE!**

. . . then the same thing happens the next time you get some money, and **you are BROKE. Again.** And again. And again.

NOW—Follow Rule No. 1. Pay Yourself First.

What's that mean? **Treat your savings like it's the first bill—the most important—you have to pay!**

What happens when you Pay Yourself First?

1. You get some money.

2. You pay your most important bill first—**YOUR SAVINGS**. Then you pay your other important bills such as rent, food, and utilities. And there are always more bills, even some you can't pay.

3. There's no money left. **But you are not BROKE!**

You've got money. You've got your savings. You are taking control of your financial life. You can make decisions for yourself.

You work hard for your money. **Don't you deserve to keep some of it?**

Take Action

Follow the Rule! It's simple. Treat your savings like it is the most important bill you have to pay! Typically, people plan to pay for "essentials." Then, they tell themselves, they will save any money that's left over. *There is NEVER any money left over!*

Apply Rule No. 1

The first, most important bill you pay every time you get money is your savings. Pay that bill first! Then pay for food, rent or mortgage, medicine, clothing, and other essentials, plus a few extras. As usual, there won't be any money left over—but—*YOU HAVE YOUR SAVINGS!*

Reasons to Save

Saving starts with your *emergency fund*. That's the money you need to have on hand in case you have to pay for a car repair, a doctor's visit, or some other unexpected expense. Your emergency fund will be small at first, so you'll have to work to build it up. Start small. Get your emergency fund in place. Then focus on your other savings accounts.

- Retirement savings. (It takes a long time to save enough money to stop working and live a decent life. You must start saving now!)
- Saving for major purchases. (A home or a new vehicle.)
- Saving for recurring expenses. (Gas, electric, phone, taxes, and similar bills.)
- Saving for a vacation. (A trip to Disney World costs one arm and one leg.)
- Saving for holiday and anniversary or birthday gift-giving. (You know a year in advance that the expenses are coming.)

Create Separate Savings Buckets

Bucket is the highly technical word accountants use to describe separate accounts they use for income, expenses, and other kinds of financial categories. It's a useful word when you think about your savings: filling up those buckets. You could use jam jars or envelopes, but modern online banking allows you to create separate "buckets" in your online bank account. Separate savings and checking accounts. Holiday shopping "club" accounts. Money market accounts. Certificates of deposit. Learn how to create separate places to store your money online. Be sure to have a special bucket for your emergency fund.

Glossary

banks; certificate of deposit (CD); credit union; emergency fund; fixed costs, fixed expenses; liquidity; living expenses; money market account; passbook savings account; pocket money; recurring costs; savings account; savings buckets; spending plan; variable costs and expenses; windfall

klee-SHAY
rhymes with
SHE MAY or SQUEEZE PLAY

Caution

A few readers may look at some content in this book and call it cliché. They'll sniff, look down their noses, and try to cast doubt on its value.

A cliché? What's that?

Cliché

cli·ché

/klēˈSHā/

1. a trite phrase or expression that has been used so often that it no longer has much meaning and is not interesting. Also: the idea expressed by it.

2. a hackneyed theme, characterization, or situation.

3. something that has become overly familiar or commonplace.

4. things that you will read in this book.

So. How is it that something becomes a CLICHÉ? Well, it's just this: People say it over and over and over and over and over and over again.

And *why* do they say it over and over and over and over and over . . . again?

Well, sometimes **it's because it's true!**

Just because it sounds familiar and seems obvious—just because it's a cliché—that does not mean it's **NOT true**.

Maybe it's a generally agreed upon **DARN GOOD IDEA**.

Maybe it's something we can call **WISDOM**.

Rule No. 2

If You Want to Have More Money, Spend Less.

Rule No. 2: If You Want to Have More Money, Spend Less.

Hey! Didn't you say you wanted *to keep* more of the money you earn?

You said you thought you **DESERVE TO KEEP** some of that money?

STOP GIVING IT AWAY!

No, it's not easy. Business in the U.S. today is all about marketing, advertising, social influencing, and guilting people into buying *stuff*. Then businesses look for more ways to get your money with subscriptions and rentals and fees and extras for add-ons and more *stuff* that you don't need **and may not even know you are paying for**.

Businesses spend billions of dollars every year on services, strategies, schemes, tricks, content, messaging, and influence peddling designed to encourage you to give them your money! They are smart and savvy, and they know more about you than you can possibly imagine. They can get right inside your head. They know exactly what buttons to push.

You, my friend, are outnumbered and outgunned in every possible way.

Fight back! Stop paying for *STUFF* you really don't NEED!

Be a cheapskate. Be a miser.

Yes, you have to pay to put a roof over your head. You have to pay for food. Lifesaving meds. Check. Check. Check.

Everything else? It's just *STUFF*.

STUFF that big companies want you to buy so they can take your money.

No cable TV? You'll live. No fancy new car? (We'll talk about that!) No new cell phone? You'll get by just fine. No bling? Oh, gosh. What will someone say?

No designer jeans? No fancy kicks? No baubles and bangles? You'll live.

You deserve to keep more of your money.

If you want to have more money, **SPEND LESS!**

Take Action

ny time you make a purchase, ask yourself: *Is this something I need or just something I want?* And remember, **the surest way to be certain you have more money is to spend less!**

Apply Rule No. 2

- Answer the question: What is the worst thing that will happen if you do not spend this money or make this purchase? Will someone die? Will someone be homeless? Will you get in legal trouble and possibly be arrested or be fined? Will someone be sick? Will you miss time at work or lose your job? If the answer is "no," then you may be spending on a *want* and not a *need*.

- Are you purchasing something new that you can buy used? Are you buying something because it has a well-known "brand"? Are you buying something because it is cool or because a friend owns it or because a celebrity endorses it? **Don't spend your money.** You worked hard for it. **Keep it for yourself.**

- Are you buying something because you are an addict: drugs, alcohol, nicotine? Use your desire to have more money to help you beat your addiction. ***Do the math. Calculate how much money you could save in the next year if you don't spend money on your addiction.***

- Are you paying the lowest possible price? When you need to buy something, shop for it. Compare prices. Don't be an impulse buyer.

- Remind yourself, every day, *if you want to have more money, spend less!*

Reward Yourself for Spending Less

Put the money you don't spend in your savings buckets. And give yourself a reward—put a little bit of it in one of your "fun" buckets—put it toward a vacation or holiday spending or buying that big screen TV.

Don't try to be a saint. Just go for really, really sane.

Glossary

Cheapskate; consumerism; do the math; drip spending; drip saving; envelope system; needs vs. wants; tightwad

The Rules

Drip, Drip, Drip: Little Stuff Matters

A leaky faucet—just a little drop every little while—doubles your water bill. That little drip, given enough time, will fill a swimming pool.

People in business understand this. A wise shopkeeper might tell you to "take care of the pennies, and the dollars will take care of themselves."

Modern merchants are all about getting that little bit extra. The banks want you to keep your balance low so they can charge you a monthly fee. The cable TV business is stacked with little add-on charges—a cable box, maybe, and a cable modem, and an extra charge for something they never explain and you never asked about.

One large segment of the stock market business today—high-frequency trading—is conducted by buying and reselling stocks in milliseconds (not seconds, mind you—one thousandths of a second). And in return, if their systems are working correctly, they may earn a tiny fraction of a mil (one tenth of a cent). And by doing this millions of times every day, they make lots and lots of money.

If you want to have more money, plug up every little leak. Watch your pennies. You can put that drip, drip, drip to work for you filling up your savings accounts.

Do the Math!

Say you spend five dollars on a fancy cup of coffee every work day. And you buy a lunch for about eight dollars instead of brown bagging it. That's nearly $3,500 a year. And in 10 years—let's do the math—$33,800! A new car. A down payment on a place to live!

Do the math!

$$\begin{array}{r} \$5 \text{ coffee} \\ \times 5 \\ \hline 25 \\ \times 52 \\ \hline 50 \\ 125 \\ \hline \$1,300 \end{array} \qquad \begin{array}{r} \$8 \text{ Lunch} \\ \times 5 \\ \hline 40 \\ \times 52 \\ \hline 80 \\ 200 \\ \hline \$2,080 \end{array} \qquad \begin{array}{r} \text{Total} \\ 1,300 \\ 2,080 \\ \hline 3,380 \\ \times \ 10 \\ \hline \boxed{\$33,800} \end{array}$$

How Needy Are You?

I need cable TV.

Boring Stuff!

No, you do not NEED cable TV. **You just WANT it.** If you didn't have it, you wouldn't get sick and die. You wouldn't break any law by not having it. If you live within 50 miles of any stations, you can get along just fine with free over-the-air TV and free movies from your library. We can talk about Internet access and streaming—that's getting pretty close to being a need these days. But cable TV? Boring Stuff!

I need a new car.

Boring Stuff!

Depending on where you live and work, you may legitimately need a set of wheels. Yes, that will mean extra costs for insurance, tags, maintenance, and your license. Make sure you catch all the drip, drip, drips. **But a NEW car?** Only if you've got the cash to pay for it and plan to keep it for at least ten years. Otherwise? Boring Stuff!

I need to take my kids to Disney World.

Boring Stuff!

No, not a need. *No way.* If you want to take a trip to Disney World or anywhere else, and you have saved the money to pay for it, then you have every right to do what you WANT to do. But don't take on any debt to do it! (See Rule No. 4). You think you *need* to go to a resort or take a cruise? Boring Stuff.

I need a pack of cigarettes.

Boring Stuff!

No, you don't need cigarettes. You need nicotine. You crave nicotine. You are addicted to nicotine. This one is difficult, but if you can do it—break your addiction—you can save hundreds and maybe thousands of dollars a year. You can save your lungs. **You can save your life.** Along with the quit smoking aids, classes, tricks, and other means you use to try to kick the habit, think about keeping your money for yourself. Do the math. **These big companies are making billions by getting people addicted to their nicotine-laced products.** And their customer addicts pay with their money and their health? That really is **Boring Stuff!**

Rule No. 3

Teeny Tiny Baby Steps.

Rule No. 3:
Teeny Tiny Baby Steps.

Think about a child—a baby—learning to walk. First a child learns to pull itself up and stand while holding on to a table or someone's hand. Then there's a flop. Baby falls down. Then a pull up, and baby learns to stand up longer. Later the child learns to take a few steps while still holding on. Then there is a first step into open space, followed by a soft landing on the floor. And then the child tries again, and again, and again, each time gaining confidence.

Pretty soon the kid is running around everywhere, and you're just trying to keep up. (Ah, parenthood.)

It All Starts with Baby Steps.

You want to save a million dollars for retirement. **How do you start?** Write a check to yourself for $100,000 and go on from there? Probably not.

You start with a dollar or maybe just some loose change.

Then add a few dollars more. You get to a hundred, and then a thousand, and you continue to build.

Sometimes, you fall down. You make a mistake. There's an emergency expense. Your savings get smaller. But if you are persistent, you can recover, get back up, and keep moving forward.

When it comes to your money, start with baby steps. Set small, achievable financial goals. Teach yourself to be successful, one baby step at a time. This is called planning.

Take Action

Think about your current situation. Do you have an emergency fund? If not, get one started. Set a modest goal—maybe just $10. Work hard to achieve that goal, and then set a new, slightly higher goal. Maybe $100. Achieve it. Keep moving forward, one step at a time. **Remember: teeny tiny baby steps!**

Apply Rule No. 3

- Get started now. Open a banking account if you don't have one. Set a nice, easy, achievable goal. One small step.
- Decide how big your emergency fund should be. Maybe a month's worth of all your expenses? Experts recommend six months, but maybe a smaller step to start. Now, divide that by the number of pay periods you have in a year. Maybe that can be your first target—your first baby step. Set up a special account—a bucket. Start filling it. Keep at it until you reach that next baby-step goal.
- Start saving pocket change. At the end of each day, put your pennies, nickels, and dimes in a jar or a piggy bank. When it is full, add it to your savings.
- Do you have a 401(k) plan where you work? Does your employer match any of your savings in it? If yes, sign up for the plan and save at least as much as your employer will match. (More about this with Rule No. 7.)
- Remember: Rule No. 1! Remember: Rule No. 2!
- What? You say you can't do it? That is Boring Stuff!

Reward Yourself for Achieving Your Goals

Think about something that you will enjoy and make that one of your savings goals. Apply Rule No. 3. Move forward one small step at a time.

Glossary

401(k) plan; fixed costs; flexible spending account (FSA); keeping score; SMART goals; recurring costs; tax-advantaged; variable costs; vesting

Boring Money Games

FSA, IRA, Roth IRA, EITC, 401(k), 529 plan. . . .

Yep. Boring, **but this is not Boring Stuff.** If you've got a decent job, this stuff goes with the territory. So buckle down. It's a game. Figure it out. Learn how to play and how to win.

In many workplaces there are tax credits and "flexible spending" accounts and 401(k) and blah, blah, blah. . . . It's all really, really boring. And for most of us, the savings are small—just a few cents here and a dollar there.

But remember the drip, drip, drip. And Rule No. 3—Teeny Tiny Baby Steps. A penny here and a dollar there and pretty soon you've reached a goal. You're ready to set a bigger one.

If your company has someone in charge of benefits, talk to them. And keep talking to them until you understand how this stuff works. Because—here's the important thing—it can save you some money! Maybe not a huge amount right now, **but every penny counts.** And once you understand all the requirements and regulations—once you **learn to play the game**—you'll be an experienced veteran. You'll be better prepared for the future.

Pay attention. Do your homework. Study the glossary in this book. If you don't understand something, find someone who does. Get them to explain it to you like you're five years old.

Rich people hire people to do all this work for them. If you're not rich yet, then you've got to do it yourself.

Learn how to play the Money Game.

Keeping Score

Here's the most interesting (and kind of fun) thing about playing money games.

It's easy to keep score.

Just look at that number in your savings account. Is it getting bigger? You're getting ahead. You are a winner in the savings game.

Keep an eye on the total in your retirement IRA or 401(k) account.

Are you saving for education? How's it going?

Are you dealing with debt? There's a number you want to see getting smaller.

Home mortgage? Watch that "home equity" number get bigger. What can you do to help it grow faster?

Yeah—for better or worse—when you're playing the Money Game, it's easy to keep score.

Take Action

- Decide what number or numbers are most important to you.
- Start keeping score using any tools you have at hand.
- Automate your finances. See Rule No. 6. Consider using a tool like mint.com to keep score.

Danger* [1]

Taking advantage of the personal benefits that you receive by observing the following rule *and keeping more of your own money* may cause severe damage to the U.S. economy.

If 27.6 percent of all Americans follow this rule, it may cause a recession. If 34.65 percent adhere to it, the country may slide into a depression. If only 12.6 percent of the American population follow the rule, it will cause a slowdown in the automobile industry and possible layoffs.

Bottom Line: *If you decide you want to keep more of the money you earn, you may be responsible for destroying the American economy!*

Is it worth the risk?

Darn right it is! It's your money!

*This Is Not Boring Stuff

Footnote [1]

The numbers and projections on this page were made up out of thin air to make a point that is absolutely true. The U.S. economy is highly "leveraged"— dependent on borrowing and credit. If a large percentage of Americans did stop borrowing, it would have a significant impact on the overall economy, and it would particularly affect the automobile industry. This is also a good example of fine print that shows you why you should always read all the fine print (even though you are likely never going to read all the fine print in any of those online user agreements you are asked to click on, because hardly anybody does that except big corporation lawyers who are trying to find ways to prevent you from being sneaky and getting away with anything and plaintiff lawyers trying to figure out ways to sue those big corporations).

The Rules

Rule No. 4

Never Pay Interest. Always Earn Interest.

Rule No. 4: Never Pay Interest. Always Earn Interest.

Let's start with the easy stuff. Let's begin with Credit cards—the quick and easy way to buy things.

But only if you **NEVER PAY INTEREST!**

When the credit card bill comes due, you pay it off, in full. No interest. No fees. No other charges. Period.

Never PAY interest.

When you pay interest, you're proving that your spending is out of control—you are spending more money than you have. As a result, you are wasting money. *You are giving your hard-earned money away.*

It's not just credit cards, either. Car loans. In-store financing. Payday loans. Any time you "buy now and pay later."

Remember: There are many ways that "interest" can be hidden.

If you pay a fee for **check cashing**, that is interest!

If you pay an **overdraft fee**—that is interest!

If you **buy a money order**, that is interest!

If you **pay to refill a debit card**, that is interest!

The **extra money you pay to "rent" something** from a "rent to own" store is interest!

This is all your money! *You are allowing people to take from you!*

Paying interest is like letting people pick your pocket. Learn to identify all the different kinds of "interest" that you may encounter—not just the obvious costs you see on a credit card bill, the hidden fees on a loan statement, or the penalties applied to late payments for fines or other debts.

Think about it. *Do you want to let people keep taking your money?* Make up your mind. **Never pay interest. Any time the word "interest" comes up, you want to be on the receiving side.**

Never PAY Interest! Always EARN Interest!

For the positive side of Rule No. 4—**Always EARN Interest**—here is the No B.S. truth: You won't earn very much. Interest income only comes in drip, drip, drips. It helps, but the "magic of compounding" is not the same powerful force it was in the mid-20th century. Read Appendix B, Earning Interest Ain't Easy, for the full story and tips on how to earn as much interest income as you can.

Take Action

Are you paying interest on credit cards now? Get those debts paid off and never let anything like that happen again! Do not let big companies take advantage of you.

Identify every unnecessary interest (or similar) payment you are making and eliminate it. The rule is simple: **Never, never, never pay interest! Always earn interest!**

Apply Rule No. 4

- First, follow Rule No. 1 so you never have to borrow money or pay fees. You will always have enough money to avoid paying interest.

- Never borrow money to buy something that loses value over time, like an automobile. It constantly gets less and less valuable. Like an automobile! (If you want to dig into the Boring Stuff, read Appendix F, Life Is Better without a Car Loan.) Appliances are another good example. Or anything else that becomes less valuable over time.

- Never incur credit card interest payments. Pay off the entire balance on a credit card every month. If you don't have enough money to do that, lock up the credit card so you can't use it. Or cut it up. Remember Rule No. 4. Never pay interest.

Pay Attention to Your Principal

A credit card or loan statement includes two numbers that you need to focus on. First, there's interest. That's the "I'm wasting my money" number. Then, the balance—the amount that you need to pay back.

With a mortgage, you pay both "interest" and "principal." Principal is your friend. The principal is the amount you borrowed and must pay back—but since you are paying for a property that you are going to own, **you are actually keeping that part of your payment for yourself.**

When you are paying down a loan for an asset that holds or increases in value like a home, you increase your *equity*—the amount of the asset that you actually own.

Paying principal is like putting money in your own pocket.

NOTE: A mortgage statement may also include charges for "escrow" (money the mortgage company uses to pay taxes and homeowner's insurance) and possibly other fees. If there is no escrow payment—or if you own your property free and clear—you'll have to pay all those expenses yourself.

Glossary

APR; compounding, compound interest; credit card; debit card; escrow; equity; fees; full disclosure; inflation; interest; overdraft protection; prepaid debit card; prime rate; principal; subprime loan; terms and conditions

Exceptions to Rule No. 4

Car Loan?

Boring Stuff! NO EXCEPTION!

A new vehicle loan is a terrible deal. The instant you drive a car away from the dealership, you lose thousands of dollars.

Your car is a machine. It has to be licensed, maintained, and insured. It loses value every day you own it and every mile you drive it. And, on top of all that, you want to pay interest?

If you really need a vehicle, pay cash for the best transportation you can afford. Maintain it well. And save the money you would have spent on payments and interest to pay for any major repairs you may need—and to buy your next car.

The only time you buy a new vehicle is when you can pay for it in full and you plan to keep it for at least ten years. See Appendix F for more about car loans and how to avoid them.

Car Lease?

Extra Boring Stuff! NO EXCEPTION!

There's a reason that a famous personal finance guru says a car lease is a "fleece." It's a rip-off. You make payments for two or three years and, at the end of the lease, **you own NOTHING!** You may even owe more money for extra miles you have driven. And—here's a kick in the pants—you get the first opportunity to BUY the vehicle that you've already been paying for. What Boring Stuff!

Remember Rule No. 1! Pay Yourself First. Save. Save. Save.

When you have savings, you control your finances. When you have savings, you don't need to cash your paycheck right away. When you have savings, your bank goes to work for you. You can write checks, transfer money electronically, and pay bills online. You don't need to worry about having cash in hand. **Everything gets easier for you financially when you have savings.**

Home Mortgage?
Yes—ONE EXCEPTION!

Why an exception? Because, unlike a vehicle, **real estate typically increases in value over time.**

You need a place to live, so you probably have to pay someone something. A mortgage payment typically includes some direct value to you (ownership equity). Depending on state and federal tax laws, you may get a tax saving based on the interest you pay on a mortgage. And, if property values go up (as they historically tend to do), you gain additional equity in the property. Increased value for real estate is not guaranteed, but at least you have a roof over your head.

A home mortgage is the one kind of debt you can consider taking on. It won't be easy though. Saving enough money to buy a place to live is difficult today. See Appendix H, The Affordable Housing Crisis.

Student Loan
Sneaky, tricky, boring stuff! MAYBE an exception, and MAYBE NOT!

For generations, conventional wisdom said that getting additional education beyond high school was ALWAYS a good idea. People with college degrees ALWAYS earned more and did better in life.

Reality check!

Today, if you need to borrow money to attend a college or university, there is significant risk involved. **You have no guarantee that getting a college degree will pay off financially.** Technical institutes and other for-profit schools are an even bigger financial risk. They advertise and sell their programs aggressively. They are **great at making promises** and signing up students—and saddling the students with loans **while failing to live up to their promises.**

Meanwhile, the cost of higher education has gone higher and higher.

And understand this: U.S. bankruptcy laws have been changed in ways that make it almost impossible to cancel student loan debt. When you take out a student loan today, you can expect that it will follow you for the rest of your life until you pay it off. **With interest!**

Deciding whether you should borrow money for education (take out a student loan) is a big, complicated question that requires a long answer. If you or someone in your family is considering taking out a student loan, be sure to read **Appendix E, Education and Avoiding the Student Loan Trap.**

The Rules

Seven Steps for Getting Out of Debt

Jamaal, the main character in the book *The Richest Man in New Babylon*, has a big problem. He is deep, deep in debt. One of the people who helps him deal with the problem and start to turn things around is the credit manager at an auto parts store—a man whose job it is to be sure the store's customers pay their bills. This is what Jamaal learns.

1. If you have dug yourself into a deep hole, **stop digging!**
2. Face up to it. **Write it all down!**
3. Pay **something** every time a bill comes due.
4. **Communicate.*** Maybe you can negotiate. **Do not be a DEADBEAT!**
5. Learn about bankruptcy and find out if that's an option. Prioritize your debts. Be sure you understand what the worst thing is that can happen if you do not pay a debt. Everyone wants to be paid immediately. **You have to decide who, when, and how much!**
6. Bust your ass. Get another job. You can do anything for long enough to get past this time in your life.
7. Repeat, repeat, repeat.

*Communicate.

This is a seriously overlooked step in dealing with debt. The people who work in collections are human beings, too. If you communicate with them regularly, call them if you miss (or know you are going to miss) a payment, and generally treat them with respect, they *might* be very helpful to you. A person at the IRS might tell you about a tax forgiveness plan. Someone at a utility might tell you about a special discount you qualify for.

If you treat someone like they are the enemy, how do you think they will respond to you?

If you treat someone like a decent person who is doing their job—treat them with respect—how do you think they will respond to you?

Take Action

Know your rights!

Bill collectors can **NOT** call you at all hours, and they are **NOT** allowed to harass you. Visit the Federal Trade Commission website. Learn about your rights.

Although there are unfair and unjust fees and practices related to incarceration, there are no debtors' prisons in America today. Learn your rights. You can also learn a lot by speaking with a bankruptcy attorney, and the first meeting is usually free.

Some debts can ultimately be ignored. You can take a "charge-off." It will affect your credit report for a few years, but then it will go away.

Communicate. Know your rights. Know what can you safely ignore. Know how to report abusive bill collection practices. Read Appendix D, Dealing with Debt Collectors.

Prioritize Your Debts

When you write everything down, you must include the total amount you owe and interest rate (if any) that you are being charged. Now, which debt do you try to clear first?

You could pick the one with the highest interest rate. It is costing you the most. Or you might decide to pick the smallest total—just so you can **feel like you are making progress**.

Either choice may be a good decision. **It's up to you.** Figure out a plan of attack that works for you and stick to it. Get to work on those get-out-of-debt steps, ending with step 7. Repeat. Repeat. Repeat.

Credit Reports and Credit Scores

Bad news: If you ignore a debt, it will affect your credit score. Good news: Credit scores don't matter to you financially unless you are applying for a mortgage. Bad news: Some employers check credit reports before hiring people. Good news: Some states are passing laws that businesses cannot do that unless the position is directly involved with company finances.

If you have questions about credit reports and credit scores, read Appendix C, How to Check & Correct Your Credit Report. The information in it is related and relevant. And remember: All of this is work you can and should do yourself.

Glossary

bankruptcy; credit freeze; CFPB; charge-off; credit counseling; credit report; credit score; deadbeat; debt consolidation; FICO; FTC

Rule No. 5

Practice! Practice! Practice!

Rule No. 5: Practice! Practice! Practice!

How do you learn to play a musical instrument? Find instruction in the proper techniques, and practice, practice, practice.

How do you learn to play a sport? Master the required skills, and practice, practice, practice.

How do you learn to cook? Develop the needed expertise in techniques, and practice, practice, practice.

How do you get better at your job so you can earn more money?

It's the same answer. Maybe a little more complicated, and yet it's pretty much the same thing. You have to figure out what skills employers value. What kind of expertise do they need? You have to look for opportunities for growth. Identify the capabilities your employers need, and practice, practice, practice.

Get a Little Bit Better Every Day

Get better at your job. Be engaged. Be dependable. Learn new skills. Practice them. Get better. Perhaps, after careful consideration and research, you find classes you can take or a license to pursue.

What do physicians do? They **practice** medicine. What do you call a doctor or an architect's business? A **practice**.

Work on getting better in the rest of life, too. Cooking and cleaning. Fitness—enjoy yourself and improve your health.

To develop any skill you need to do two things. First, learn the action involved. What is the proper form—the right stance to hit a baseball, the right heat on the stove to cook an egg, the right forms to collect and fill out to complete your taxes. **Then—*you practice, practice, practice.***

You need exercise to take care of your body, right? You need exercise to take care of your money, too.

Every day you get another opportunity to work out with your money management skills. Shape up your saving. Trim that spending. Strengthen your self-control.

When managing your money, keep getting better all the time. Better at saving. Better at reducing your spending. Better at planning. Practice, practice, practice.

Get a little bit better every day!

Take Action

Think about everything that you do. Are there things you would like to improve? Make a list of possible areas for self-improvement. Decide which ones to pursue. Consider which ones may be easiest, so you can have early success. Think about which ones will give you the greatest benefit, so you will feel motivated to succeed.

Apply Rule No. 5

- Pick two or three important aspects of your life. Make one about taking care of your money (Rule No. 1). But pick one or two other areas, as well. Develop a plan (teeny tiny baby steps) for each one to get better.

- Is there a way to track your success with measurements? Improved free throw percentage? Increased savings? Keep score. Are you practicing regularly? Are you succeeding? What are the results?

- Are there job skills you can develop that will help you succeed financially? Education and training opportunities that can open doors for you?

- Is there a free or inexpensive class you can take at an adult school or an extension? Maybe job-related, or maybe just something that interests you.

- **Use your library card!** (You do have a library card, right?) **Read books!** (Audiobooks are great for commuting.)

Things never stay exactly the same for us. We'll talk about that later in *The Rules*. For now, just remember that if you aren't getting better, then you are either stagnating or getting worse.

So get going. Start practicing!

Glossary

certifications; coach, coaching; cooking; exercise; for-profit schools; keeping score; practice routines; student loans

Rule No. 6

Make It Automatic.

Rule No. 6: Make It Automatic.

Computers take better care of your money than you do. Seriously, computers are your best financial friends.

How's that? *They help you keep your hands off your money!* Cash is dirty and carries germs—and worse, it's oily and slick, too. It can slip through your fingers!

Credit cards and debit cards are slippery, too. Computers can give you an edge in managing them.

Bottom line: **Automate your finances.** You want to be as hands-off as possible when it comes to handling your money.

Living in Today's E-conomy.

Everything—not just money management—is being automated. Job applications, car registrations, buying concert tickets, and ordering pizza—you have to be prepared to do it all through some kind of computer interface. Business in America is all about doing things faster and cheaper. It might not be better, especially if you've got questions, but that's how it is.

You're living in the American E-conomy. Take advantage of it when you're taking care of your money.

You're paying for all the computers and electronic services offered by banking, credit card, investment, insurance, and similar companies. They all offer computer access to your information and the tools you can use to track your money and manage it better. **So, do your homework.** Educate yourself. Explore all the free tools they offer. **And USE THEM.**

Automate everything you can. Keep your hands off your money and let the computers do the work for you. When you are in full control of your money, you can put your finances on automatic pilot. You can use free online services like mint.com to monitor your money and help you keep score.

> **Banks vs. Credit Unions?**
> You need modern banking services, but you might not need a bank. You might be better off with a credit union. Large, modern credit unions offer all the same products and online services as big banks. Credit union accounts are insured by the NCUA the same way bank accounts are insured by the FDIC. What's the difference? Read about them in the Glossary and read Appendix K, Credit Unions versus Banks. Then consider your options.

Take Action

Select a bank or credit union that has **excellent** online banking services, **but be careful!** Study all the terms and conditions for your account carefully. Understand the rules for minimum balances, fees, and penalties.

If the institution offers overdraft protection, **be absolutely positive you understand how it works.** For example, if you don't have enough money in your account, does it (a) decline the transaction or (b) accept the transaction and then charge you a fee and maybe some interest, too? **(Option B is NOT acceptable.)** Read the Glossary entry on overdraft protection.

Apply Rule No. 6

- Do research on banks and credit unions. Even if you currently have a bank account, it may not be the best one for you to use. Talk to friends. Read recommendations. **Do your homework.** The financial institution you choose can have a major impact on your financial future.
- Join a credit union, or establish an account at a bank with excellent automation and online services.
- If you can get direct deposit for your paycheck, sign up for it.
- Automate your retirement savings. If your company offers a 401(k) plan, sign up for it and contribute at least as much as your company is willing to match. You end up with a small, automatic deduction from your paycheck that you'll barely notice. **Remember:** *This is retirement fund money—nothing else! Do not neglect your emergency fund and other savings.*
- Automate paying your bills. Set up automatic text or email alerts to notify you about deposits, withdrawals and low balances.
- Make your savings plan(s) automatic. Set up separate accounts (buckets) for savings, and make regular deposits to them automatically.
- Set up online access to all your credit card, 401(k), banking, mortgage, investment, and other financial service accounts. Use the login information to view all your financial information in an online budgeting and tracking account like mint.com.

Glossary

account number; ATM; autopay; bank; budget, budgeting; credit cards; credit union; direct deposit; FDIC; friction; gift card; NCUA; overdraft protection, prepaid debit card; prepaid (secured) credit card or debit card; routing number; vesting

Rule No. 7

Investing & Insurance = Legalized Gambling.

Rule No. 7: Investing & Insurance = Legalized Gambling.

Buy a lottery ticket? You know the odds. There's a one in a zillion chance you'll become a millionaire. There's a really good chance you wasted a dollar.

Bet on a ball game? Or a horse? Maybe someone told you about a sure winner? Ten bucks might win you twenty. Maybe you're out ten bucks—but you know you had a better chance of winning than when you bought the lottery ticket. Bet five dollars on the flip of a coin? Maybe you'll win. Maybe you'll lose. Fifty-fifty chance.

Making investments? Buying insurance? That's just another kind of gambling.

You ante up—buy a stock, pick a mutual fund, or pay an insurance premium. The people you're gambling with tell you the odds.

When you make an investment, maybe you'll win. Maybe your bet will pay off and the investment will grow in value. *But it may not—they tell you that!*

Insurance? It's the same, but different. What are the odds something bad is going to happen? **With most insurance, you're making bets you hope to lose.**

Car insurance? You don't want to have a wreck, but if you do, you'll have money to deal with repairs or replacement of your vehicle. Life insurance? "Winning" is "not dying." You may have lost a little money, but you protected your family just in case. And if worst comes to worst, you've given people you care for some financial protection.

Health insurance is different, because it provides up-front benefits. Checkups. Preventive care. Plus, it can save you from unpredictable but genuinely catastrophic medical expenses.

Companies that sell stocks, bonds, and such call their business *investing*. Companies that sell insurance call it *risk management*.

Deep down, under the buzzwords and lingo, it's just gambling. You figure out the odds. You make a bet. You hope that you'll win. Sometimes you lose. **One thing to remember**—in gambling, investing, and buying insurance—is that you're dealing with sharp, experienced people and businesses. Their products and services are set up so that, over time, **they will always earn money.** There's a term for this, too.

The house always wins!

Ridge Kennedy

Take Action

Analyze every investment or insurance purchase as though you are a professional gambler. Think about the odds (the chances you will benefit), the potential payoff, the worst case if you lose, and the rake—the amount of money that other people involved in the transaction are taking.

Apply Rule No. 7

- Keep your eyes open. Keep asking questions until you are sure you understand how an investment or insurance policy works. **Read ALL the fine print before you sign anything.**

- Never sign an agreement the same day it is presented to you. Read the fine print again. Get second (and third) opinion.

- If you are working with a sales representative, be sure to ask how the sales representative is compensated. **There is no free advice when you are talking to a sales rep.** Always remember: If you ask for advice from sales representatives, *they are 99 percent sure to recommend you buy what they sell!*

- *If something sounds too good to be true, it usually is!* Any time you encounter a *great* opportunity, you need to double your efforts to find a hidden catch. If you proceed, you need to be sure you can afford to lose the entire amount and still be okay financially.

- Guard yourself against scams and schemes. Protect yourself against identify theft. **Do not give anyone your personal information** like your Social Security number and date of birth unless you are absolutely sure there is a legitimate need for that information **and you initiated the communication**. If you have even the slightest doubt, keep your information to yourself.

- Remember—the house always wins. Nothing in business is really free.

Companies that sell insurance, investments, pari-mutual bets, and lottery tickets are all in the same business. The only differences between them are how much you'll be paying to play and your odds of winning.

Glossary

deductible; diversification; identity theft; IRA; portfolio; premium; risk averse; risk management; risk/reward; risk tolerance; sucker bet; term life insurance; whole life insurance; vigorish (vig)

Hedging Your Bets

When you hedge your bet, you do something to reduce and prevent losses, just in case things don't go the way you hoped they would. "Hedging" is a big deal in the world of high finance. There are massive "hedge funds," for example, that professional investors use.

But even if we don't have millions or billions to work with, we can still take steps to protect ourselves from massive disappointments. That's why the following ideas are important. **Pay attention.** In our world of teeny tiny baby steps, **these are things that matter**.

Risk Tolerance and Risk Aversion

If you put $10,000 into a stock market bet and it loses 10 percent of its value, how are you going to feel? If you can say "that's okay, I understand. It's the stock market. It goes up and down. I'll roll with it"—then you have a *high tolerance for risk*.

On the other hand, if you are going to feel terrible and try to get your money out of the investment as quickly as possible and put what's left in a nice, warm savings account—you are *risk averse*.

If you work with investment advisors, they **should** help you determine your "risk tolerance." You can find many free risk tolerance assessment quizzes online. Taking a few of them is a good way to learn more about investing (legal gambling) and risk.

Diversification

Don't put all your eggs in one basket. One stumble—you've got an omelet on your hands.

The same wisdom applies to investing. When you make your bets, don't go all in on one investment—one stock, fund, or other asset.

A "mutual fund" automatically spreads a stock market investment over a group of companies. That's a start in diversifying your portfolio. Most 401(k) plans offer mutual funds that invest in bonds and in real estate, as well as stocks. Professional investment advisors say that you should include them in your investments.

You'll see information about how a fund has done in the past. You'll see warnings that say this past performance does not ensure future returns. Maybe you can find someone you can trust who will advise you. Maybe you'll just guess. **But if all your money is invested in one or two stocks, that's probably not a good idea.** You may want learn more about diversifying.

Risk Management

Don't bet over your head. If you're uncomfortable with investing, there are low-risk options. Savings accounts and CDs won't earn you much interest, but they are safe bets. You'll find higher interest paid by online banks backed by reputable companies like Goldman Sachs and American Express.

More on Investing & Insurance

A Basic Investment Plan

The most common investment decision you're likely to make is how to distribute your savings in a 401(k) plan or an IRA. Typically you'll be presented with a selection of a dozen or more investment options. You will be asked to "allocate" some percentage of the money in your account to one fund or another until you reach 100 percent. You'll have access to information about the past performance of the funds and be warned that doesn't predict how they will do in the future. Honestly, if you're like me, you won't understand much about all this. And you have to make some choices.

Welcome to the wonderful world of investing!

Your options will probably include some kind of money market fund—the equivalent of a savings account. A money market fund will not lose value; nor will it earn very much interest.

You'll then see a variety of different options.

Talk to the experts who manage your plan. Determine your risk tolerance. **Make some choices, and hope for the best.** If you find the process interesting, learn more about it. There are endless resources online and there are some books listed in the Resources section of this book.

If you find the process stressful, annoying, or simply Boring Stuff, read Appendix G, Investment Advice from a Rich Man. It offers straight talk on investing from one of the wealthiest people in the world.

A Basic Insurance Plan

Insurance is really, really Boring Stuff. Unfortunately, it's also *IMPORTANT Boring Stuff* that allows you to protect yourself and the people you care for.

Health Insurance. You need it. It's your "hedge" against the devastating impact of huge medical bills. If you don't get health insurance from your work, look at the plans at healthcare.gov. *Yes, if you live in the United States, you need healthcare insurance!*

Term Life Insurance. If you have dependents—people who will be greatly affected economically if you die—then you should consider having **term life insurance**. The younger you are, the less it costs. If you're healthy and don't smoke, you can get a lot of coverage for a small price. **It's a cheap bet that you don't want to win—and it provides security for people you care about.**

Car Insurance. In most states, you are legally required to have insurance. If you don't, you risk losing your license and possibly being arrested. Uninsured drivers are guilty of fiscally reckless driving.

Rule No. 8

Things Never Stay the Same.

Rule No. 8: Things Never Stay the Same.

"**H**ow's it going?" someone asks. "Same old, same old," you reply.
No!

Things never stay "the same."

Our environment changes, the stock market ticks up or down, tides ebb or flow. Every minute brings you one minute closer to the end of your life.

(Cliché alert!)

The only thing that is constant is change.

Most of the changes we experience will be good. Growing more financially secure. Making new friends. Accomplishing goals.

But it's likely there will be unexpected tragedies, too. Illness. Death.

Even if you are young and healthy, you have a responsibility to yourself and the people around you to plan for the future. Just in case.

When you take insurance and retirement savings into account, you may be surprised by the amount of money involved. But more important, by doing proper estate planning, **you take a huge burden off the people around you.**

When the worst happens and someone dies without a will (called *intestate*) there are laws in place. The estate goes into "probate" and a set of rules is applied. Any outstanding matters will be sorted out and any assets or possessions will be distributed according to those rules.

But is that what you want?

Wouldn't you really rather talk to the people closest to you and **make those decisions yourself?**

Hey, it's just the truth. Things never stay the same. Illnesses happen. We have accidents. And eventually, we are all going to die. So take action, make decisions for yourself, and remove a burden for the people closest to you.

It's not easy, thinking about this sort of thing. But it's the right thing to do.

Take Action

Look into the future—for you and the people closest to you. Where are you going to be in five years? Ten years? Twenty years? And what about all the other people close to you?

If you are getting out of debt or building your first emergency savings fund, you have to apply Rule No. 3—Take Teeny Tiny Baby Steps. Live life one day at a time.

Occasionally, though, you need to step back and look at the big picture. Consider your hopes and dreams, for you and the people around you. Consider the realities of life, difficult subjects such as illness, accidents, and death.

If you want to have control over your life, you must do some of this kind of planning!

Think about your personal assets—if you were to die suddenly, who would you want them to go to? *If you were seriously injured and unable to communicate, who would you want to help make medical decisions for you?*

Apply Rule No. 8

- Obtain an estate planning worksheet and fill it out. (Search online for "estate planning worksheet pdf" to find lots of choices.) See how much information you have on hand or in your head. You will probably find you have a lot of additional information you need to track down.

- Create a will for yourself. Free tools are available to help you do this online at sites like freewill.com. Get started—**get something in place**.

- Create a living will. What happens if you have a serious medical condition or injury? If you can only survive using mechanical devices, should that continue? Who will make those decisions for you?

- Plan to have an attorney review your will and living will to make improvements or corrections if they are needed for the state where you live.

- Be sure your documents are properly signed and witnessed. Inform people who are directly affected, like your executor. Once you have created your will, tell the people closest to you where it is. Just. In. Case.

This is difficult!

Facing up to your mortality—thinking about dying—**is hard!** Seriously, though, think about how you want to be remembered. Think about the people YOU want to remember. Think about making life so much easier for them.

This is your legacy. Don't you want to have your say in it?

Glossary

executor; living will; estate or inheritance taxes; intestate; power of attorney; probate; will

The Rules

CLICHÉ ALERT

Uh-oh.
More Painfully Obvious Stuff.

Yes, Painfully Obvious.
But it is
NOT
Boring Stuff.

Rule No. 9

The Most Important Things in Life Are Free.

Rule No. 9: The Most Important Things in Life Are Free.

It's a corny cliché. It's not fit for a pop song lyric or even for a greeting card.

But—damn it—it's true.

Good health. The love of a child. A beautiful sunrise. Sharing time with a trusted friend. A walk through falling leaves on a crisp, cool fall day. Your faith. A peaceful night's sleep. All free.

Serenity doesn't cost anything.

The world around us is filled with commercial messaging that is telling us what we should need or should want. People selling "stuff" are trying to tell us what is cool, what is hot, and what we should run out and buy right now. All this messaging—advertising, marketing, and sales pitching—it's all about money.

Our economy seems to depend on having us exchange our hard-earned money for lots of "stuff." And we are supposed to believe that once we have that stuff, we will be happy.

Is that true? Can money buy happiness?

We call B.S. on that—Boring Stuff!

Money is important. We need to have enough money to meet our basic needs. When we don't have enough money, it makes life much more difficult—more stressful. But is money the most important thing in life?

Consider all the things that are most important to you, and think about how many of them do not have a price tag.

Take Action

Stop. Reflect. Think about everything in life—the big picture—and your hopes and dreams. What is really important in your life? What makes you happy? What makes you sad?

Do you attend a house of worship? If so, make a visit some time when you can be alone. Sit and reflect. Let your mind wander. Count your blessings.

Make a list. Start off with something like "the three most important things in my life that are free." Think about your answer. Write it down. Now, can you think of some more?

Apply Rule No. 9

- Take your first list of important things that are free and reorganize it and rewrite it. Make some additions. Post it where you see it every day.
- Start a gratitude journal. Get a notebook. At the end of every day, write down three things from the day for which you are grateful. This helps you become more aware of the little things—things that, for the most part, we don't pay for—that make us happy and enrich our lives.
- Learn about meditation—also called *mindfulness*. Take a class if you can. Or you can start looking up meditation videos on YouTube.

Stop and smell the roses.

(Yes, it's a cliché. You were warned.)

Seriously though, if you can sleep through the night in a warm bed with a roof over your head, you are blessed. If you can wake up in the morning, put your feet on the floor and stand up—you are fortunate. If you can watch the sun rise, you're lucky. Health. Friendship. Love. A spiritual connection. Birds singing. A nice day. Don't take all of these things for granted. They are part of your great wealth.

Glossary

advertising; branding; faith; gratitude; marketing; mindfulness, meditation; spirituality

Valuable and Free: Your Reputation

Personal Relationships

Being a good person doesn't cost you anything.

Listen—really listen—to other people. Imagine seeing things from their perspective.

The Golden Rule exists in some form in every religion and ethical value system: **Treat other people the way you want to be treated yourself.** With respect. With compassion.

If you anger easily—if you get into verbal disputes or physical fights—you have a serious problem. Consider the Golden Rule. There are resources to help you reduce your anger and find peace. Draw on them. Seek help!

Your reputation is free—but it is not cheap. Nourish and protect it.

Angry Online Relationships? *Don't Be Stupid!*

When people get online, something bad happens. Without the calming influence of face-to-face interaction, some people become LOUDER and GET ANGRY and SHOUT. They "like" and repeat ANGRY and OFFENSIVE things.

DON'T BE STUPID!

If you say something online, **you should assume it will be there for anyone in the world to see FOREVER!** That stupid thing you said five years ago may sabotage your search for a new job. An offensive remark from 10 years ago could spoil a current relationship. A slur you posted online 20 years ago might cause you to be fired!

Live your life online as though it will be permanently recorded and remembered. Seriously, **DON'T BE STUPID ONLINE!**

Business/Commercial/Financial Relationships

Live up to your commitments. If you are working on paying down a debt, keep in communication with the lender. When you stop communicating, you will be labeled a DEADBEAT. **Don't be a DEADBEAT!**

Your Relationship with Credit Reporting Agencies

The importance of credit reports and credit scores is greatly exaggerated. Except for this.

Some employers, sometimes even without permission, check a job applicant's credit report before making a hiring decision. And **some landlords** check a potential tenant's credit report before renting or leasing them a place to live.

And then, someday, you may be **applying for a mortgage** or a business loan, and at that point your credit report may matter.

So, it makes sense to be sure that if someone checks your credit report, it is as accurate as possible.

Check and Correct Your Credit Report

Read Appendix C, How to Check & Correct Your Credit Report. Study up. Learn the terminology, the precise meaning of the words related to credit reports and credit scores. Make sure you have the necessary identification information. For most people, that's your Social Security number and date of birth. Follow the instructions.

This is a process you can and should do yourself! It takes a little while and it is tedious. It is, in fact Boring Stuff! But it is easy and straightforward, and you can do it. You do not need to *pay someone else to do it for you!*

Your Relationship with the Law

If you get a court summons concerning a debt (or anything else), find out exactly what it is about. **DO NOT IGNORE IT.** Show up in court—even if you can't afford a lawyer. If you are a no-show, *you are sure to lose*. If it's a debt-related case, you will allow bill collectors to pursue you, armed with legal judgments. Courts can give them the ability to take money out of your paycheck or withdraw money from your bank account.

Show up in court, and at least you've got a chance to make your case. And you will know what legal rights the bill collectors have to take your money.

Net Worth? Net Worth. Net Worth!

Sounds impressive, doesn't it?

Occasionally you'll see advertisements for financial services that are offered to **"high net worth individuals"** or **"high net worth investors"** and people like that.

They even have an acronym. Check out HNWI on the Internet. You'll find references to people who have at least a million dollars in liquid assets and who are definitely in demand. The casino industry has a term for HNWI who like to gamble. **They're called** *whales*.

Here's the problem: *"Net worth" is not a term reserved for rich people.* It's for everyone. And when it comes to keeping score, your net worth is (cliché alert) the bottom line.

No, It's Not!

The *No. B.S. Rules* encourage you to crunch the numbers. Get to the bottom line and figure out your net worth—for yourself and for your family unit. **It's important to have the facts.** Knowing your net worth will help you make better decisions when you must make them and better choices when you have options.

Add up all your assets. Subtract all your debts. You end up with a number: your net worth.

Net worth is important, but it's just a number. You can use it to keep score. But still, it's just a number. What happens when you consider it in relation to Rule No. 9?

Net Worth+PLUS

> *Not everything that can be counted counts*
> *and not everything that counts can be counted.*

The words above are frequently attributed to Albert Einstein. Maybe he said them, and maybe he said them first. And maybe that's all a story and someone else deserves the credit. That does not change the fundamental wisdom of the message.

When you calculate your net worth, think about *everything* **you've accomplished.** Your trajectory. Your momentum. Add to that the value of everything you've done that doesn't show up on a balance sheet.

Think about the good things you've done that you never asked for or received credit for. Being a good parent. A good friend. A good work colleague. A good teammate.

All of that counts!

Crunch the numbers, for sure. Then give yourself the extra credit you deserve, as well. Calculate your **Net Worth+*PLUS***.

Take Action
Calculate your own Net Worth+PLUS.
1. Get a dedicated notebook or select an online finance tracking program. See the Resources chapter for recommendations.
2. Link to or list all your banking accounts, credit card accounts, loans, old debts you are paying down—everything.
3. At the same time every month, log in or do the math. Calculate your monetary net worth. If you have a mortgage, be sure you track the equity in your residence—the amount you actually own vs. the total amount due (with all that interest).
4. Create an online spreadsheet or use pages in your notebook to track the results, month to month. Keep score.
5. Think about Rule No. 9. Write down a few of the many good things you can add to your net worth that can't be counted or calculated on a spreadsheet.
6. Look at the numbers. Consider the good work. Figure out your Net Worth+*PLUS*.

Celebrate
- Congratulate yourself. Maybe have dinner with someone close to you. Keep tracking your Net Worth+PLUS monthly. **And listen up—even if the news isn't great**—maybe your net worth numbers go down a little bit—at least you are making the effort. You have the courage and intelligence to do the work, and **you know what the heck is going on!** That is a **big deal** all by itself!
- Think about the results. Apply Rule No. 3. Teeny Tiny Baby Steps. Maybe a new goal? A higher target. Keep moving. One small step at a time.
- Net worth, the way accountants define it, is about money. **Net Worth+PLUS is about more than money.** *It is about Wealth!*

Dollars and cents matter. Now you have another way to measure, another way of keeping score, and you can work on it. But there's much more to life than that.

You are—no doubt about this—a wealthy person. Think about that.

Glossary
asset; debt; equity; interest; liability; net worth; principal; spreadsheet; underwater

Rule No. 10

It's All up to You.

But...

Rule No. 10:
It's All up to You.

Whether it is saving money, completing your education, getting a new job—whatever challenges you are taking on—your success is up to you. You must take responsibility for the outcome of your efforts. And you must accept the reality that there are no easy answers.

Be sure you understand what accountability means. It is about you, personally, taking charge of yourself and your actions. There's no boss to write you up or teacher to give you a bad grade. You cut out the middle man. You decide what you want to accomplish. Then you make sure the job gets done. That's accountability.

It *Is* All up to You—But You Don't Have to Do It Alone!

Yes, it's your responsibility. You are the who is accountable. But that does not mean that you have to do it all by yourself. You can and should have a support team around you—your family, your friends, people you work with, professionals you have confidence in, and other reliable people you trust.

Talk to people. Share your concerns—you'll find others who feel the same way. Celebrate your successes—even if they are only teeny tiny baby steps.

Maintain your connections with good people. Work at this. And **build up relationships with new people**—people who are reliable, caring, and connected to you or your community.

The term *networking* is used in business. It refers to the way that people who know people (who may know other people) tend to get new job offers or new clients. In today's world, with its social networks and online job applications—the idea of networking is even more relevant and important.

Business groups. Associations. Investing clubs. Book groups. Bowling teams. Softball leagues. Religious studies. Exercise classes. Etc., etc., etc. You get the idea—any time people get together in a friendly, supportive environment. **Get out and participate** whenever you can.

Get connected! Work at it!

And remember: **Attitude is everything.** You need to be positive and upbeat. There will be times when you really don't feel that way—so put on a show. "Fake it till you make it"—that's what they say. And when you do that, you'll find that pretty soon you start to believe it yourself.

Take Action

Gather up your resources. Build your team. Identify family members and friends you can talk to who will be supportive. Find mentors. Smart people. Experienced people. It's human nature—people want to help and to give advice. Seek them out. Listen.

Recognize that you will face a lot of challenges, and that you may fall short sometimes. Don't get discouraged. But be determined to succeed.

Apply Rule No. 10

- Have a family meeting with the people closest to you. Talk about your goals. Talk about how you can support each other in achieving them. Hold each other accountable for getting it done—whether it's saving money, quitting smoking, or washing the dishes. Take responsibility. Be accountable. Celebrate your success.
- Volunteer to help others. Find an organization that is helping people less fortunate than you, and help them out. Make a small financial contribution if you can. But even better, volunteer your time and energy. **Help other people.**
- Engage with other people in your community. Join a club. Volunteer for a job. Play a sport. Get connected with new people.
- Follow the Golden Rule: Treat other people the way you would like to be treated.
- It is more important to give than to receive. **Believe it!**

Look in a mirror. **You are looking at a wealthy person!** You see someone who knows **The Rules**. You see **a person who is taking control**—managing money and not letting money manage them.

You see a person equipped with the tools to make sound financial decisions. And that's not Boring Stuff.

Glossary

celebrating success; fiduciary; mentor; tracking your success

In Conclusion

This is it. The end. No more rules. No Boring Stuff.

Do you want to have more money?

Do you want to have fewer financial worries?

Follow the rules!

It may not be easy at first. It may not ever be easy.

You will face pressure!

Big business—*they want your money.*

Family demands—*they want and may really need your money.*

Friends and acquaintances—*they want you to have fun, be a good sport, and spend your money.*

But listen up!

It may not be easy at first, but **you can do it.**

There will be setbacks. Don't give up. Follow *The Rules*.

The Rules can take you to a place where you can be comfortable—where you can stop worrying about money and focus on more important things.

Maybe you will decide that having more money is an important goal. After you bank your first $50,000 in savings by following *The Rules*, you will have a solid foundation to build on. And as you build, you will discover that you're are still following *The Rules*.

When you don't follow *The Rules*, you will know exactly how and why you are not. You'll understand the risks and rewards.

Knowing The Rules will still help you make better, wiser decisions.

And for the rest of us, following *The Rules* just keeps life simple so we can stop worrying about money and get on with the more important things in life.

The Rules

Rule No. 1. Pay Yourself First.

Rule No. 2. If You Want to Have More Money, Spend Less.

Rule No. 3. Teeny Tiny Baby Steps.

Rule No. 4. Never Pay Interest. Always Earn Interest.
Paying principal puts money in your own pocket.

Rule No. 5. Practice. Practice. Practice.
Get a little bit better every day.

Rule No. 6. Make it automatic.

Rule No. 7. Investing & Insurance = Legalized Gambling.
Remember: The house always wins.

Rule No. 8. Things Never Stay the Same.

Rule No. 9. The Most Important Things in Life Are Free.

Rule No. 10. It Is All up to You.
But you don't have to do it alone.

Part III

The Appendices*

***Appendix**
ap·pen·dix
/əˈpendiks/

plural **appendixes** or **appendices**

1. a small tubular sac with no known useful function attached to the large intestine.

2. a section or table continuing additional information added to the end of a book

CAUTION
Boring Stuff!

To be read only in event of actual *SERIOUS INTEREST* in the topics under discussion.

DISCLAIMER: The following pages, from here to the end of this book, are ***not covered*** by the No B.S. Warranty.

Claims of Boring Stuff on any of these pages will be automatically disallowed.

The Appendices

Appendix A: The Emergency Savings Fund Crisis

Appendix B: Earning Interest Ain't Easy

Appendix C: How to Check & Correct Your Credit Report

Appendix D: Dealing with Debt Collectors

Appendix E: Education and Avoiding the Student Loan Trap

Appendix F: Life Is Better without a Car Loan

Appendix G: Investment Advice from a Rich Man

Appendix H: The Affordable Housing Crisis

Appendix I: Cryptocurrency and NFTs

Appendix J: Savings and Retirement

Appendix K: Credit Unions versus Banks

Appendix L: Can You Trust the Stock Market?

Appendix A

The Emergency Savings Fund Crisis

Internet news sources are filled with surveys and statistics about Americans and their failure to save.

Here are some samples.

> *"Two in five Americans have less than $1,000 in savings."*
>
> *"Six in ten Americans don't have $500 in savings."*
>
> *"A growing percentage of Americans have no emergency savings whatsoever."*
>
> *"One in four Americans have no emergency savings, survey reveals."*

It's not just Americans.

> *"In the UK, nine percent of Brits have no savings, while over 40 percent of people do not have enough put away to support themselves for a month in the absence of income."*

The result of all of this, in addition to providing lots of blaring headlines, is that people are forced to make important financial decisions under duress. When something bad happens—the car breaks down or a child gets sick—they may do things they would not do if they had money readily available.

Emergency expenses **are never unexpected.** You *know* they will occur. The only problem is **you do not know exactly WHEN they will occur**.

What kinds of things are people forced to do? Maybe it's putting an expense on a credit card that results in paying a lot of interest. Maybe it's worse—taking out a payday loan. Maybe it's a personal sacrifice—going without your medicine so that you can afford medicine for your child. Maybe it's borrowing money from a person you think is a friend—who turns out to be someone who abuses friendships.

If there is one, and only one, thing you take away from this book it must be this: Pay Yourself First. Obey Rule No. 1. Create an emergency saving fund for yourself so that you are not forced to make a bad decision because of the kind of common, ordinary emergency expenses that happen all the time.

Appendix B
Earning Interest Ain't Easy

For the first half of the 20th century, saving money and earning interest was a simple proposition. There were thousands of banks, savings and loan associations (S&Ls), and credit unions. Every community had its own bank. Small towns might have two or three. Cities had dozens. Following the massive wave of bank failures during the 1930s (9,000 banks failed and more than $140 billion was lost during the decade) the banking industry *was—for a time*—well regulated.

All of these small and midsize banks competed for customers' deposits. They all paid interest at a good rate to people who opened savings accounts. Through the 1960s and into the 1970s, anyone who opened a savings account could count on receiving at least 5 percent interest. Maybe they'd even get a free toaster. That steady 5 percent interest, compounded daily and reinvested in a savings account, was enough, over a lifetime, to support someone in retirement.

Stocks could be purchased that produced a stable income. Utility stocks (gas and electric companies, especially) became known as *widows' and orphans' stocks* because they promised a steady income if the primary breadwinner of a family died.

Beginning in the 1980s, all of that changed. The banking industry didn't like being regulated. It wanted more freedom. Bankers wanted to make more money.

The savings & loan crisis of the 1980s, caused by deregulation of the S&L industry, kicked off the changes. Greedy business dealings, enabled by the deregulation, resulted in the failure of about a thousand S&Ls—a third of the industry. Despite the failure of those businesses, the banking industry was further deregulated, allowing it to expand nationally and sell more financial "products."

Big banks acquired smaller banks, and the financial services industry grew more and more powerful through consolidation. In 1983, there were more than 14,000 banks in the U.S., with more than 40,000 locations. In 2020, there were only 4,000 banks. But they had nearly 75,000 locations. In 1947, the U.S. finance industry earned 10 percent of total nonfarm business profits. By 2010, that rose to 50 percent. Over the same period, finance industry income as a portion of the U.S. gross domestic product rose from 2.5 percent to 7.5 percent, and the finance industry's portion of all corporate income rose from 10 percent to 20 percent.

As financial institutions grew bigger and even more profitable, they didn't need small depositors any more. They didn't need to pay interest for savings accounts.

And those steady, reliable, widows' and orphans' stocks? Utilities were deregulated. The anti-regulation forces said free markets would provide lower rates for consumers. Instead, we got the same rates while those stocks with reliable returns disappeared. Of course, utility executives, industry insiders, and wealthy investors made lots of money.

There is one other powerful force working to keep interest rates low: Wall Street. Big investors, brokers, financial engineers, financial managers, and top corporate executives all crave low interest rates. Why do people in the financial services industry want low interest rates?

One reason is that it allows them to purchase more stock with borrowed money (buying "on margin"). It's a risky investment strategy, but it is widely used. About 2.4 percent of the S&P 500's $38 trillion market capitalization (that's more than $900 billion) was borrowed money, according to Barron's in 2021.

NOTE: *In March of 2022, in a move to control inflation, the Federal Reserve raised its prime interest rate to 5 percent, producing a brief period when interest on savings accounts–especially at online, high interest savings banks–reached five percent. Rates have been drifting downward steadily since then and the Federal Reserve fell under intense political pressure to reduce interest rates in 2025. When the Federal Reserve reduces interest rates, the interest paid to individual savers goes down as well. So, interest rates can sometimes go up for savers, but it is rare in the modern U.S. economy. Businesses and wealthy investors prefer low interest rates and they typically get what they want.*

But wait. There's more.

Low interest rates are especially valuable to "private equity" investors (formerly known as *corporate raiders*). One standard practice they employ after taking control of a company is to borrow huge amounts of money that pay back to themselves (management fees, their original investment, and stock buybacks that increase the value of their shares). Low interest rates facilitate this, allowing them to borrow more money and load their target companies up with more debt.

What does all this mean to ordinary human beings?

It means that earning money on your savings is difficult. Interest rates for savings accounts have been close to zero since 2008.

The financial services industry wants to force you to invest money in securities (stocks, bonds, mutual funds, and similar financial service industry offerings). **The people who run these businesses are not going to reward you for following Rule No. 1—for being a saver.**

However, if you want to be a saver, there are ways you can fight back.

For people who are risk averse, there are banking options such as high-interest online savings accounts that provide more interest than ordinary accounts. Promotional rates for certificates of deposit (CDs) are sometimes available. Money market accounts may earn a little more interest, but they are not government insured.

The money you save by NEVER paying interest makes up, in part, for the small return that you get in interest on savings.

You can take investment advice from one of the world's most successful businessmen and invest with great caution and minimize your risk. Read Appendix G, Investment Advice from a Rich Man.

A relatively complicated but safe option is available through the Treasury Department's TreasuryDirect savings bonds. You can purchase Series I savings bonds (think Series I for Inflation protection) with variable interest rates or Series EE bonds that have a fixed interest rate. These modern savings bonds are all-electronic (no paper certificates) and have conditions and limits. Learn about them online or talk to your financial advisors for more information.

Finally, if you are looking for someplace to get that old fashioned 5 percent return on your money, you can receive a little bit of it through some credit card rewards programs.

Credit card issuers have been offering airline miles, points, and other rewards for a long time. If you follow Rule No. 4 and pay off your account in full every month (never pay interest) you can earn some money back through these programs. The high percentage rate cash back offers come with lots of conditions and limitations, including caps on the amount you can receive and restrictions on the types of businesses where you can receive higher cash back percentages.

If airline mileage programs seem too complicated (they are) and reward points programs seem to be another form of marketing (they are), you can keep it simple. Look for the highest possible cash back percentages, and use credit cards intentionally, according to the best rewards deal, especially when making purchases at supermarkets, pharmacies, automotive service stations, and travel and dining businesses. You may end up playing a money game, using one card for food and another for gas and a third for dining. But if you follow *The Rules*, you can emerge a tiny bit ahead.

In a supermarket, you might see the customer in front of you in a checkout line open an envelope and pay in cash. Then, when you pay for your groceries with a credit card and receive a 5 percent discount, it seems unfair in a way.

It is unfair. The system is rigged. But this kind of situation highlights the benefits of following *The Rules*. Saving money gives you the resources to make financial choices. And following *The Rules* allows you to earn a small benefit when you spend your hard-earned money.

The financial services industry is about one thing: maximizing its profits. But there are small ways that you, as a consumer, can benefit. Play the game when it works for you. But always follow *The Rules*.

Appendix C

How to Check & Correct Your Credit Report

The importance of credit reports has been magnified, purposely mystified and then repackaged into products that businesses large and small try to sell you. The clearest example of this is found at the freecreditreport.com website.

In 2003, the federal government required the credit reporting industry to provide people with a free copy of their credit report. The credit reporting industry has made every effort to turn this into a profit-making opportunity. And so we get websites like freecreditreport.com.

If you log in to the website, you get information from *one* of the three major credit reporting companies. You also get offers *to purchase information* from the other two credit reporting companies. And you get offers to purchase services to monitor your credit report—to let you know if anyone requests your information. Then you start receiving email messages telling you that your credit score has gone up or down, offering another service for you to buy.

If you are an ordinary person who simply wants to be sure the information on file is correct and your financial position is being accurately reported, you don't need any of this stuff.

How much will you have to spend to clean up you credit history and improve your credit score?

The price of a few postage stamps and envelopes.

Here is what you actually need to know and what you can do. First, understand the lingo—the words and terms used in the credit reporting industry. Next, be sure you have the personal identification information you need. Finally, follow a few simple steps to get copies of your reports for you to review. Then, if there are errors on the reports, get them corrected.

Understand the Lingo: The Language of Credit Reports

Language, lingo, jargon—it's all just words. Be sure you understand what each word or phrase means. It makes a difference when you are working through this process.

Credit Bureau: There are three major companies that provide credit reports in the United States: Equifax, Experian, and TransUnion. There are other companies in the business, but these three are the biggest and the ones that matter most. In conversation, they are called credit bureaus, credit reporting agencies, consumer reporting agencies, or credit reporting companies. For this book, we are going to call them credit bureaus.

NOTE: There are dozens of smaller companies that are in engaged in the *screening* business. They collect your personal information and sell it their customers. Most familiar, perhaps, are companies that provide reports on prospective tenants to landlords. Some firms provide screening services for medical, insurance, banking, utility, gambling, and other businesses. Employers may use credit bureaus and screening services. Companies that provide screening reports may draw on records from the national credit bureaus as well as data from other sources—criminal records, for example.

All of these companies are covered by the Fair Credit Reporting Act. You are entitled to see a copy of their report on you at any time. If someone takes an adverse action against you based on one of their reports (you get turned down by a landlord, for example, or rejected for a job), you are entitled to request and receive a free copy of the report. And you have the right to dispute any information on these reports. For more about this, visit the Consumer Financial Protection Bureau (CFPB) website and search for information about "consumer reporting companies."

Credit File: The major credit bureaus collect personal data about individuals from banks, credit card companies, utilities, stores, public records, court records, and other sources. Today, the data collection is all automated and stored on the credit bureaus' computers. All of the data about an individual is included in the person's "credit file." A person's credit file may include information about the person from birth to death.

Credit Report: A *credit report* is a selection of information from a person's credit file that is provided to a credit bureau customer (or to an individual requesting their own credit report). There are legal limitations applied to the data that may be included in a credit report. For example, a request for a credit report itself (a "hard inquiry" or "hard pull") will appear on a report for two years. A delinquency (late payment), a charge-off (failing to pay a debt in full) or a mortgage foreclosure will appear for seven years. Therefore, after the appropriate time, the negative information should no longer appear on a person's credit report. A bankruptcy can appear on a credit report for up to 10 years, depending on the specific kind of bankruptcy. As of April 2018, tax liens and civil judgments are no longer supposed to appear on credit reports.

So, what is a credit report?

A credit report is a selection of data that is drawn from an individual's credit file that is maintained by a credit bureau. There are legal requirements that determine what information can be included in a credit report. There are not, however, any legal requirements for credit bureaus to actually delete data from their credit file.

Credit Score: The idea of a *credit score* was invented by a company now known as FICO. It provides its customers with an easy way to decide whether a potential customer is a good risk. Instead of having to read and interpret all the information on a credit report, the credit score sums up the data in one number. Decisions about credit eligibility and interest rates are simplified. And the new credit score is perfect for automated systems.

Now FICO has been joined by VantageScore, a competing business providing credit scores that was created by the three major credit bureaus. Credit score information is widely available at no cost from your bank, credit union, and other sources such as mint.com.

A credit score is based on the data collected by the credit bureaus. A credit score is a number from between 300 and 850. A low credit score of 300-629 is "bad." A score from 630 to 689 is considered "fair." A "good" credit score is between 690 and 719. A score above 720 is considered "excellent."

Important Point about Credit Scores: An individual cannot correct or improve a credit score directly. All a person can do is correct and improve the information in their credit file that appears in their credit report. *In order to improve your credit score, you have to correct and improve the data in each credit bureau's credit file.*

How to Check or Correct Data and Information in Credit Bureau Credit Files

Do NOT hire a company or anyone else to help you. You can and you should do this yourself.

Do everything by mail. Rely on the U.S. Postal Service. *Do NOT go online to do this.* The online free credit report website is designed for marketing. If you give it an email address, you will be bombarded by offers for stuff you do not need.

NOTE: You can also request a free credit report by phone. It is better than doing it online, but it is a long, tedious process. Making your request by mail is easier. However, you can call 1-877-322-8228 and follow the voice prompts to order a free credit report. The first thing the message will tell you is to go online. Wait and you will get options for doing the process by phone or by mail. At the very end of the automated call, you will get an option to choose which credit bureau reports you want to receive. You can also choose to get reports from all three credit bureaus at once.

The No B.S. Process for Checking Your Credit Report
The Information You Need Before You Start

The most common identification used for credit reporting is a person's Social Security number and date of birth.

NOTE: If a person does not have a Social Security number, it can be difficult to get credit report information, but it is not impossible. Other identifying information, such as the addresses of places you have lived, bank accounts, credit card accounts, and phone bills or utility bills may be used. (Generally, this only applies to non-U.S. citizens who are living temporarily in the United States.)

The Process

1. Go online and search for "free annual credit report request form." Download the form and print it out. Also, visit the Federal Trade Commission website (ftc.gov) and read the article Disputing Errors on Your Credit Report. It gives detailed information about this process.

2. Complete the form. You will need your Social Security number and date of birth. You *can* request credit reports from all three major agencies.

Recommendation: If you are not under time pressure, do this process one credit bureau at a time. Start with Equifax. Alphabetical order. Follow the steps below. Then move on to Experian and TransUnion.

3. Mail the form to the address printed on the form.

4. You will receive a copy of your credit report in a few days. Go through it carefully. Identify any errors. Is your name misspelled? Are any past addresses incorrect? Are there bank accounts or credit card accounts listed that are incorrect? Is an ex-spouse or even a total stranger listed on an account? Identify any incorrect information on the report.

NOTE: If you disagree with something on the report, you can dispute it. The credit bureau has the responsibility to verify anything you dispute within 30 days, as long as the matter is not "frivolous." If the people at the credit bureau cannot verify the information, they are required to remove it.

5. Send a written request for corrections to the credit bureau. Include copies of the reports with corrections marked on them and any backup information you can provide. Keep a copy of everything you send. Each credit report you receive should have a mailing address where you can send dispute letters. You can also look up the mailing addresses online.

6. The credit bureaus are required to respond to your request within about 45 days. If your request results in a correction, you are entitled to receive a new copy of your credit report. You have additional rights. You can ask the credit bureau to send corrected copies of the report to companies that requested a report recently, including people who got a copy for employment purposes. Check the FTC website article for more details about this and other steps such as your right to place a statement concerning a dispute with a creditor on your credit report.

7. Repeat the process until you are satisfied the report is accurate. Then, if you are doing one credit bureau at a time, repeat all the steps above for each of the other credit bureaus.

NOTE: You will find a great deal of good additional information about this process online. The Federal Trade Commission (FTC) has a comprehensive guide available in a printable PDF format. It includes sample letters, the request form, detailed information about the applicable laws, and more. Visit FTC.gov and search for *Credit Repair: How to Help Yourself.*

NOTE: The information you see in reports provided by credit bureaus is **NOT ALL the information they have in your file**. There are no legal requirements for the credit bureaus to DELETE information. States and municipalities are generally moving toward restricting the use of credit reports by prospective employers, with a constantly changing patchwork of laws and regulations. However, with all the companies that are involved in the screening business, you can never be absolutely certain what information is or is not available.

Appendix D

Dealing with Debt Collectors

Our advice here is simple. Do your homework! Start with a visit the Federal Trade Commission website (ftc.gov). Search for information about debt collectors and your rights. You are protected, by law, against abusive practices. Study up. Learn your rights.

Then, visit the Consumer Financial Protection Bureau website (cpfb.gov) and read the information provided there about your rights, what debt collectors can and cannot do, recommendations for arranging a settlement of a debt, and more.

On the cpfb.gov website, search for the free, downloadable document "Know your rights when a debt collector calls." It provides a summary of important information and links to more detailed assistance. The two-page document is available in English, Spanish and at least seven other languages.

Know your rights!

Do not allow yourself to be harassed or intimidated.

Do Not Let Bill Collectors Get the Legal Upper Hand

This is very, very important: If you receive any kind of legal papers like a court summons, **you must NOT ignore them**. Debt collectors use the legal system to obtain judgments and the right to take money from your paycheck (garnish your wages) and even to take money from your bank account.

If you fail to appear in court, debt collectors will receive a "summary judgment." **They win. You lose. Automatically.** And you will not have any more warning about what is about to happen.

If a bill collector does obtain a judgment, you can go back to the CFPB and FTC websites to get information about how that may affect you; what they can and cannot do when armed with a judgment.

You have rights that you can exercise even if you are not represented by a lawyer. **Do not close your eyes and just hope it all goes away.** Take advantage of the information available from the CFPB and FTC.

Know your rights!

Appendix E
Education and Avoiding the Student Loan Trap

BIG PICTURE: Spend as little money as possible on postsecondary (after high school) education. If you or your student wants to pursue a four-year college degree, start with two years of less-expensive community college. Then transfer to an in-state public college or university to complete your degree. **SAVE YOUR MONEY.**

WARNING: For this strategy to work well, students must understand how community college credits will transfer to a four-year college. Four-year colleges do accept credits from community colleges. The catch is: Do those credits fulfill the specific course requirements for the degree the student wants? Frequently, students earn a large number of community college credits that may not fulfill the requirements for the degree they want to pursue. That could mean they need an additional semester or year of study. If you are planning to transfer, be sure to study the degree requirements. If you are going to make a course correction and change majors, do it at the less-expensive junior college level. Know where you stand with your credits in your planned major.

BE AWARE: A typical four-year college degree today has a value similar to that of a high school degree a half century ago. A college degree is expected by many employers, but earning a degree guarantees nothing. While college graduates may be searching for jobs, individuals with special skills, such as computer coding, may earn big salaries even if they do not have a college degree. Such cases may be uncommon, but they are examples of the "no guarantees" of postsecondary education.

Upon obtaining a four-year degree, many students realize they need an additional year or two or more for an advanced degree in some field of study. **Therefore, SAVE YOUR MONEY for when you are really going to need it.** By the time students are planning to attend graduate school, they will be more focused, and the odds of getting a reasonable return on their investment in education will be much higher.

WARNING: The following information is very basic and generalized. Student loans are a $1.75 trillion business that is constantly growing and changing. There are hundreds, if not thousands, of lenders and more than 45 million individuals with student loan debt. If you are of an age to be considering student loans for yourself, a child, or another close relative, you ought to be sufficiently Internet-savvy to explore the information available online and get up-to-date details about loan programs, requirements, and some of the pitfalls this book describes. Our objective, if you continue to read the information that follows, is to make you aware of the extreme risk imposed by student loans and to encourage you, if you must take on this kind of debt, to do so very, very carefully and only if absolutely necessary. **Student loans are easy to obtain, difficult to manage, hard to repay, and nearly impossible to**

discharge in bankruptcy. *Do NOT let yourself or your family fall into the student loan trap.*

Education Is the Answer. Now, What Was the Question?

In the United States, the idea that higher education will provide the answer to many of our nation's most challenging problems is widely accepted. There's just one problem. *It's not true.* Here are a few questions followed by an answer you might hear.

How do you make sure children are successful in life? Education!

How do get ahead at work? Education!

How do we, as a society, overcome inequality and prejudice? Education!

If you don't have a lot of money, what is the one thing you can borrow money for and be sure you will be able to pay it back? Education!

Boring. Stuff.

Education is an important resource people can use to solve problems and get ahead in life, **BUT NOT AT ANY PRICE!**

Education—specifically postsecondary education—has changed significantly and become much more expensive since the end of the Second World War and the era of the GI Bill. Once upon a time, a college degree was a reliable path to a good job and a better life.

Unfortunately, the "once upon a time" story was not true for everyone in the 1940s and '50s. The G.I. Bill (post WWII) discriminated against Black soldiers from the South. The benefits were administered by state governments and were not made widely available to Black veterans in southern states.

Today, the "education is the answer" story has become more myth than fact for EVERYONE!

It is true that many students, probably a majority, benefit from postsecondary education. They may, however, graduate with a large student loan debt—a financial burden that can have a major impact on their futures. It is also true today that a large number of students who enter postsecondary education programs fail to complete their studies or fail to benefit, even if they receive a degree or certificate. They are left burdened with debt that they may never be able to pay off.

And yet, the "education is the answer" myth remains powerful and pervasive.

Why?

It is promoted by politicians and government sources because it sounds like a plausible answer to difficult problems. It is promoted by the education industry because it keeps schools in business; it puts students in classroom seats. And the myth is gratefully supported by the student loan industry. It keeps them in business and makes them a great deal of money.

As a result, parents and students, with all the good intentions in the world, are being lured, hooked, and reeled into a student loan trap.

What all these people should be saying is this: Education is the answer, as long as it is at the right price.

Reality Check

Colleges and universities are big businesses. They offer a service—education—that, when purchased in the right quantity, provides students with a product: a degree. The retail price of a year of education service at a typical four-year college or university ranges between $25,000 and $75,000. Therefore, one of those degrees runs you anywhere from $100,000 to $300,000.

That is very expensive! So the college and university industry has successfully lobbied the government for money to help students pay for college (to buy their product). Some money is available through grants—free money that doesn't have to be repaid. But most of the money that is offered to help students buy education comes in the form of student loans. The government and colleges make it very easy for students to get lots and lots of money in loans to help pay for education products.

For-Profit Education

When a big pool of money becomes available, enterprising private business operators take notice. Business schools and trade schools have existed nearly as long as colleges and universities. But with all that money available—the government grants and loans—private, for-profit education became much more profitable and much more aggressive in seeking out students who were not attending colleges. The for-profit schools offered opportunities to study technical subjects or trades and earn certifications. Then, the for-profit industry even began operating for-profit college and university programs.

Here is what you are looking at today. Thousands of education businesses—some nonprofit and some for-profit—are actively seeking customers (students). They all have marketing departments actively recruiting customers (students). The marketing effort creates a picture of a beautiful educational experience and suggests that the customers (students) will receive great rewards for their education purchases in the future (high-paying jobs).

The Financial Aid Department: Right Arm of the Sales Department

Since education products at either a nonprofit or a for-profit business are expensive, all of these businesses have financial aid departments. The purpose of a financial aid department is to show the customers (or their parents) how they can afford to pay for the products the education businesses are selling and, in some cases, even arrange student loans for them.

Financial aid departments at schools are exactly like the finance departments at auto dealerships. The car dealer finance person's job is to show customers how they can borrow money and buy a new luxury SUV. *Financial aid departments exist to help customers go into debt to purchase a degree or certification.*

Educational financial aid departments actually have an extra advantage over a car dealership. The "finance person" at a car dealership has only the information on a credit report to use to assess a potential customer's needs and bargaining position. The education industry asks for more.

Most education businesses require their customers to complete a Free Application for Federal Student Aid (FAFSA) form. The FAFSA detailed financial information from the student and family. Applicants for federal loans must complete the FAFSA.

Private colleges may also require students to complete a College Scholarship Service (CSS) profile. The CSS, operated by the College Board, charges a fee to complete the profile plus a fee to send it to each college an applicant selects. The CSS is used by the colleges to distribute financial aid money they control.

Because of these financial disclosure requirements, college financial aid departments have a much stronger bargaining position when dealing with their customers (students). They know more, so they have the ability to make their offers more appealing to help them close the sale.

The education industry financial aid experts will identify the free money first—the grants. Then they may identify work opportunities that will allow the customers (students) to work and earn some money. Then, if they want to make the product more affordable, they will offer discounts (scholarships). And finally, they will make up the difference by recommending student loans.

Here's the most important thing students and their families need to be completely aware of. Education businesses (nonprofit or for-profit) are all working hand in hand with the student loan industry. They all benefit (keep their jobs and earn more profit) by encouraging students to take on student loan debt. They are not lying awake nights worrying about what it will take to pay off that debt.

Welcome to the Student Loan Jungle

Customers (students) can apply for federal student loans or private student loans. There are subsidized and unsubsidized federal loans. Parents can also take out federal loans. Interest rates for federal loans vary from year to year and are set by Congress. Sometimes they are very low (3.75 percent in 2021) and sometimes they are higher (up to 6 percent in recent years).

Private loans are offered by banks and other profit-making businesses. The choices are endless, and they may allow customers to borrow extra money to cover living expenses. Private student loans are frequently "securitized"—a financial services industry device that turns the loan into an investment in the same way that mortgages were "securitized" before the 2008 housing bubble and economic recession. This means the loans are broken up into smaller amounts, bundled into investment securities, and sold to investors. As a result, the original loans may now have dozens or hundreds of owners. If you are the person who took out the loan, you do not have anyone to go back to and hold accountable if there are problems.

Additionally, federal loans can be "consolidated" and refinanced by private, for-profit companies. There are lots of companies that want you to do that. Once a loan is refinanced, maybe it can be refinanced again, or maybe not.

If a federal loan is refinanced, you may lose a valuable benefit—loan forgiveness. If you are struggling to pay off a loan and have been dealing with bill collectors, a refinancing may restart the statute of limitations on the loan and allow bill collectors to restart their collection process.

The one thing you need to remember through all of this loan and refinancing business: The companies are all making money. They are not doing this to benefit students or their families; they are doing it to earn more profit.

Here's a summary: The federal government and lots of companies are willing to loan customers (students) money that will not have to be repaid until after the time when the customer (student) is supposed to graduate. It will feel like you are getting free money. It will feel good. In today's student loan market, nearly anyone can borrow enough money to pay for a college degree or professional school certification. Then, about six months after graduation, the customer (student), and possibly the parent or another relative who was foolish enough to cosign for the loan, will have to start paying that loan back.

How Much Debt?

The short answer is lots. An undergraduate in 2022 can borrow up to $57,500 in federal loans. Graduate students can borrow up to $138,000 in federal loans. The average college student graduates with about $30,000 in student loan debt. That's an average. For every student who graduates debt-free, there's a student with $50,000 in debt or more.

What Is the Guaranteed Return on Your Education Investment?

Nothing.

You earn your degree. You receive your certificate. What is it worth? That's up to the job market. The degree or certificate may qualify a student for certain employment opportunities. Or it may qualify a student for further education investments (an advanced degree of some sort). But remember this: Degrees or certifications do not guarantee any return on education investments.

Worst Case Scenarios

Many students (and their families) manage to pay off student loan debt successfully. But some do not. Why is that?

In some cases, it may be due to unrealistic expectations. Spending up to $100,000 on a degree in a notoriously low-paying field, such as art history or literary criticism, can lead to big trouble.

But what about the case of the business major who only has $20,000 in debt? The student gets a good job and starts paying off the loans. But then the ex-student's company is acquired, and the ex-student loses the job. It takes several months to find a new job. The ex-student misses some payments. There are penalties and additional interest. A new job is found, but the ex-student still has to keep up with rent and pay for food. Then the new job doesn't work out, and more payments are missed.

The $20,000 debt balloons to $30,000 or $40,000. The ex-student tries refinancing. Now the loan payment is smaller, but it will take 20 years or more to pay it off.

The agreement terms for some federal loans include a benefit that will cancel the balance of the loan after 20 or 25 years. The refinancing of a federal student loan eliminates that possibility.

Over the course of the loan, the ex-student will pay much more in penalties and interest than the original $20,000 that was borrowed. And there's no way to escape this debt. It is nearly impossible to discharge student loan debt in bankruptcy.

What happens now? Do the ex-student's parents drain their retirement savings to help their child? Do they put their own futures at risk?

Welcome to the student loan trap.

Warning: Loan Forgiveness and Loan Servicing Companies

Companies that collect payments are central figures in the student loan industry. Making loans and spending money for education is the easy part of the business. It is when the loan payments come due that things get complicated. There were, in 2022, seven companies that "serviced" federal student loans.

This part of the student loan industry has been especially troublesome for some borrowers. In 2022, for example, a lawsuit against Navient (a company that stopped servicing student loans in 2021) ended with a $1.85 billion settlement over accusations that it had misled borrowers into costly repayment plans and predatory loans. Loans serviced by Navient were turned over to a company called Maximus.

Similarly, a company called FedLoan Servicing, operated by the nonprofit Pennsylvania Higher Education Assistance Agency, has announced that it will stop servicing all federal loans by the end of 2022. It is transferring all its federal loans to other servicing companies. This is significant because FedLoan was the only company servicing the federal student loan forgiveness program.

The Public Service Loan Forgiveness (PSLF) program, created in 2007, promised to eliminate the remaining loan debt for federal loan recipients who made payments for 10 years (120 qualifying monthly payments). *In 2017, when people were first eligible for loan forgiveness, 28,000 public service workers applied for debt relief. Only 96 applications were approved.*

Some of the problems with the program have been corrected. Temporary measures enacted during the Covid pandemic resulted in additional loan cancellations. Still, problems with the program persist.

The lesson for student loan borrowers is this: If you think you are taking out a loan that is eligible for a forgiveness program, it is essential to study the fine print and document everything on paper. You need to maintain a print file of all documentation, because the content of websites can change. You need to be aware that multiple companies may be involved in the loan and the repayment process—your loan may be shuttled from one company to another, and information may be lost.

It is especially important to study the details for repayment plans and document your payments. You must be aware that choosing the wrong repayment plan may make you ineligible for loan forgiveness—and phone operators at the loan servicing company may not know that. Know for certain that if you "consolidate" or refinance a loan in any way, you will become ineligible for loan forgiveness.

If you think you will be eligible for loan forgiveness, you must know the program rules inside and out. Document everything you do and every payment you make on paper so that you can prove your eligibility beyond any doubt. Then hope for the best.

Conclusion Number 1

Spend as little as possible on postsecondary education. If you are following the traditional college and university route in today's work environment, you are likely going to want an advanced degree. Save money for that.

Be certain you read all the fine print. Learn about the terms for forgiveness programs, the statute of limitations for the debt, how the terms are reset with refinancing—all the little "gotcha" details that can cost you money and peace of mind.

If you're going for a certification, do your homework and be sure the education business you are working with actually delivers on its marketing promises.

The education industry (nonprofit and for-profit) wants you as a customer. Enrollments are dropping. It has to fill seats. It wants you and it is working closely with the student loan industry to load you up with debt.

You're smart. You want more education. That's a good idea. But seriously, do not be a sucker.

Conclusion Number 2

Education is wonderful. There is nothing more satisfying than working with good teachers, experiencing classroom challenges, engaging with your fellow students, and learning stuff—sometimes just for the sheer gol-durn joy of learning stuff.

For college students, or for anyone, classes in language and history and Shakespeare will enrich your life. Many classes you take may be irrelevant to the task of earning money, but they may prove to be life changing in other ways.

A great benefit of postsecondary education comes through learning how to learn. You discover how to equip yourself to adapt and change as the world around you changes—and change it will, you can be sure of that.

Education is valuable. It is much to be desired and pursued. But, at the same time, you must be careful and refuse to overpay for it, get into debt, and put yourself in an untenable financial position.

Be smart. Be wise. Be skeptical. Remember that education is a business and you are a customer. Remember Rule No. 4. Never pay interest. And if you must break that rule, do it with eyes wide open and only as a last resort.

Appendix F

Life Is Better without a Car Loan

Modern automobiles (cars, trucks, SUVs) are generally extremely well-engineered, well-manufactured machines. With proper care and maintenance, modern vehicles can easily provide excellent, reliable transportation for at least a decade and a minimum of 200,000 miles. That's a minimum. Realistically, modern cars are capable of 300,000 miles and more. The average age of vehicles on U.S. highways rose to more than 12 years in 2021. About 16 percent of all Toyota Land Cruisers have more than 200,000 miles on them, and more than 2 percent of all models from Toyota, Honda, and GM have 200,000 miles on their odometers.

With this kind of great, long-serving technology available, why is it that so many people are saddled with car loans? Today, more than a third of all Americans have car loans, totaling $1.3 trillion. Car loans account for nearly 10 percent of personal debt in the U.S. (Mortgages make up nearly 70 percent of U.S. personal debt. Student loans come in second at around 11 percent.) The average new car loan payment is about $650 per month. The average payment for a pre-owned (used) car loan is about $500.

All of those loans mean people are paying lots and lots of interest.

BUR . . . Rule No. 4. Never pay interest!

What are you going to do?

Maintenance and Machines

Let's lay the groundwork for life without a car loan. There are two key areas to focus on.

First, take care of your current vehicle properly. Maintain it. Get your vehicle maintenance manual out, look at the recommended service intervals and requirements, and invest in the proper maintenance of the machine. (Vehicle maintenance intervals and logs are generally available as PDF documents, findable with a bit of online searching.)

Oil changes. Filter changes. Tire rotation. Checking fluid levels and changing things like transmission fluid at recommended intervals. And yeah, replace the timing belt or serpentine belt when recommended. Any old belts, corroded cables, or cracked hoses—get them replaced.

You can go the premium route by getting service at a dealership. You can't go too far wrong, but you will pay more. If you have a good, independent auto mechanic you trust, you are blessed. In reality, some of the recommended services and intervals in the owners' manual are unnecessary. You and your mechanic can focus on the essentials and keep your vehicle safe and running reliably.

But wait, there's more.

When your vehicle gets an inevitable ding or scratch, get it repaired. If there's a tear in the upholstery, find a specialist who can fix it. You were backing up and, dang, a taillight was damaged. Fix it. The trunk latch isn't working correctly. You have to slam the lid. Fix it yourself or get it repaired.

And still, there is more.

Keep the vehicle clean. Whether it's you or your children doing the work or making trips to the car wash, clear up the litter and vacuum every two months. Remove stains and gunk. Keep the machine clean, inside and out, under the hood, in the cargo areas, everywhere.

And finally—the coup de grâce. Detailing.

Consider this. Once every year or two, have your vehicle detailed. Detailing is the term used for super cleaning a vehicle, inside and out. It is the kind of cleaning process that auto dealers put used cars through before they resell them as pre-owned and certified. A proper, professional detailing will make your old set of wheels feel new again.

Pay for Maintenance or Face the Much More Costly Alternative

If you really believe you need a vehicle, you've must save money (Rule No. 1) to pay for it. Skip oil changes and critical maintenance, and you may be facing a big repair bill, such as replacing or rebuilding an engine. Or worse, having a mechanical failure can cause an accident.

Even the small expenses involved in keeping your vehicle clean will forestall bigger expenses.

For example, say you have failed to maintain the vehicle. It starts having a smoke problem. Then there's a problem with a wheel bearing. It's making a sound. And there are some dents and a cracked headlight. Plus, the inside is a pig sty. It's disgusting, depressing, or both.

Let all of that happen, and suddenly you find yourself in a car dealership. And you are good and well screwed. You are about to end up with a big payment, with lots of interest, that you will be making for years. You're going to spend $20,000 or more, just because you didn't spend the few hundred dollars it would have cost annually to keep your vehicle maintained properly.

Most of the "Need" for a New Car Is in Your Head

Why is all this maintenance and cleaning so important? It helps keep you out of the "I need a new car" trap. Think about it. Your vehicle has a couple of obvious dings, and there's a tear in the driver's seat upholstery. There's the window that's not working and some other little problem. Then you have a bigger problem—the car needs a new axle or new shocks all around. Suddenly, it becomes really easy for you to convince yourself that you NEED a new car. That is, of course, Boring Stuff. But with all those little, nagging issues, it becomes very easy to fall into the trap.

Maintain your vehicle well. Keep it clean. Then you'll have a clear mind and make smart decisions when it comes to replacing or upgrading your ride.

How to Motivate Yourself to Do the Right Thing

Every time you make a car payment, imagine what you could do with that money instead.

Add more to your emergency savings? Add to your retirement fund? Save for a special vacation? Pay for some household repair that came up without dipping into emergency savings? Enjoy a special night out? Every month!

Just imagine how nice it would be to not have to make that payment!

Other Strategies to Consider

Do you actually need a car? Or a second car? There is a growing market in car sharing and car borrowing services. If you live in a city with a decent transit system and only drive once in a while, maybe a car share would be right for you. Go online and look up car sharing services.

What if you have an older, high mileage car but you want to take a special trip? Long distance. You'd like a vehicle that's a little roomier with no worries about high miles. **Consider renting a vehicle.** For the cost of one or two car payments, you can have that luxury vehicle for your trip. And at the end of the trip, you will not see payments stretching out into the distant future.

Keep Out from Underwater

You are facing the worst case scenario. You really, actually, legitimately have to borrow money to acquire a vehicle. You know that the vehicle is a depreciating asset: The longer you own it and the further you drive it, the more it loses value. You know you are going to break Rule No. 4 and pay a lot of interest.

At the very least, stay out from underwater!

You are *underwater* when the amount of money you owe for a loan is greater than the value of the thing you are buying.

Example A: You buy a new car that costs $38,500. You pay no money down and have 60 months to pay about $40,000. You are underwater the moment you drive the car away from the dealership. You rolled extra expenses into the loan. The $38,500 car was only worth $35,000 as soon as you bought it. If your circumstances forced you to try to liquidate (cash in) your asset (the car), you'd end up without a car and still several thousands of dollars in debt.

Letting yourself get underwater with a loan is a bad thing to do.

Example B: You buy a pre-owned SUV that costs $20,000. You put $8,000 down and finance the remaining $12,000 at a fair interest rate for three years. In a worst case situation, you can resell the SUV and you'll get a good percentage of what you paid. You'll be able to pay off the balance of the loan with the money you get. Yes, you broke Rule No. 4, but you stayed in control throughout the process. As a result, you are in a stronger financial position.

Lesson: Dealers make every effort to convince you to buy expensive vehicles and then persuade you to take out a loan to pay for it. They make money selling cars. **They also make money financing the sale of cars**—just like banks. Dealerships are selling vehicles AND loans.

If you must take out a car loan, be careful. Take control of the process yourself. And do not let yourself be put underwater.

A Long-Term Rental

A car lease is a fleece, especially if you drive the car a lot or you are thinking you may keep it beyond the length of the lease. However, car companies love to get buyers hooked with low mileage, low-cost leases. It helps them move cars through the dealerships, and there may be times when a lease is actually a smart financial decision.

In a situation where a reliable vehicle is needed for a short time—two years for a typical car lease—and you are confident the driver won't exceed the mileage limitation of the lease, it may be worth considering. In this scenario, however, the important thing is to remember that you are only RENTING the car. If the rent is cheap enough, maybe it's a tactic worth considering.

One Last Word on Car Loans

Because car loans are such a common consumer debt, they are heavily weighted in the calculations used to compute individuals' credit scores. Therefore, it is true that having a car loan and making regular payments on time will increase your credit score and make you look better to credit bureaus and potential lenders. With that said, successfully *paying off* a loan (without taking out a new loan) will provide that same positive data, and it will stay on your credit report for years.

You are left with a decision. Would you rather have ongoing payments (and waste money breaking Rule No. 4) along with a slightly better credit score? Or would you rather be putting more money in your own pocket? It's your call.

Appendix G
Investment Advice from a Rich Man

Warren Buffett is well known as one of the wealthiest people who ever lived. His reputation (Rule No. 9—it's free) has been that of a generous philanthropist and a person *not* given to living the lavish lifestyle of the rich and famous—a very decent human being who became very, very wealthy through wise investing.

In a letter to shareholders that Mr. Buffett wrote in 2014, he shared his recommendations for what to do with his money after he died:

> My advice to the trustee couldn't be more simple: Put 10 percent of the cash in short-term government bonds and 90 percent in a very low-cost S&P 500 index fund. (I suggest Vanguard's.) I believe the trust's long-term results from this policy will be superior to those attained by most investors—whether pension funds, institutions or individuals—who employ high-fee managers.

Later in the letter, he said:

> Both individuals and institutions will constantly be urged to be active by those who profit from giving advice or effecting transactions. The resulting frictional costs can be huge and, for investors in aggregate, devoid of benefit. So ignore the chatter, keep your costs minimal, and invest in stocks as you would in a farm.

Treat your investments as you would a farm? What does he mean by that?

Plant your money in your investments the way a farmer plants seeds. Then watch them and wait for them to grow. Like a farmer, you have to be patient. For the farmer, the process takes months—and with some annual crops or orchards, years. For investors like Mr. Buffett, the process takes years and even a lifetime.

Occasionally, you identify a crop that is failing. You may remove it and replace it with another. But generally, the good farmer (or investor) simply tends the fields and watches the crops grow.

As the first part of the quotation suggests, keep a portion of your money (he suggests 10 percent) in some safe, liquid account where it will be easily available if you need it.

In summary, one very wealthy, accomplished investor suggests putting the money you want to invest in a low-fee ("no load," in financial jargon) index fund. You are automatically diversified by being invested in a broad range of companies. Keep more of your money by spending less on fees. Reduce your risk by betting on the entire U.S. economy. And keep some money where you can access it easily—for occasional expenses and your emergency fund—just in case.

Appendix H
The Affordable Housing Crisis

Ordinary people in the United States today face extraordinary financial challenges. Income inequality is increasing. Many people in the middle classes are burdened with debt. Wages for working people, on average, are not going up. Support programs for people in need cannot keep up.

As people age, the challenges faced by Americans from the baby boom generation (born from 1946 to 1964) increasingly come into focus. Retirement is an expensive proposition. The statistical picture of savings for people 65 and older in the U.S. is grim. The average balance in their 401(k) plans is about $60,000. That's an *average*. According to some reports, a quarter of boomers may have no savings at all.

There is more bad news. If current trends in housing continue, life is going to get harder and more challenging for ordinary Americans in the future. When people create a spending plan (budget), the biggest expense they usually have to account for is shelter. Rent or a mortgage; you must put a roof over your head. Shelter, along with food, clothing, and air, is a necessity of life. Shelter has become another profitable business opportunity for wealthy investors.

Real estate has long been an area where individuals have invested and made money. A person might buy a property, turn it into apartments, rent them out, and buy more property with the proceeds. Large companies build apartment complexes and earn handsome profits. Real estate investment has a long track record of success. Even when housing prices go down, like in 2008, the market tends to recover fairly quickly and continues to go up.

Now, real estate investing has expanded into a new area: single family homes. People with large amounts of capital are looking for more ways to make money. One way to do that is to buy houses and rent them out. It's a profitable business. Deep-pocketed "institutional" investors can easily outbid local individual buyers. In some areas of the United States, foreign investors are buying homes, as well—with no intention of actually living in them.

In the past, house trailers (mobile homes, manufactured homes) provided affordable housing for ordinary Americans. Over the last few years, institutional investors have been buying up trailer parks at an increasing rate. After a trailer park is acquired, rents typically go up and the new management frequently requires tenants to make costly upgrades. Unless, of course, the new owners decide to subdivide the land into building lots and sell it to home builders.

The impact of all of this recent investment activity has been higher rents for apartments and higher prices for houses. Affordable housing has become even more scarce. People are forced to spend more for shelter. These investors have altered the character of neighborhoods, creating single family residential areas where corporate owners may outnumber individual homeowners.

Historically, the idea of buying and owning a home has been an essential part of "the American Dream." Home ownership has certainly been a very important way that Americans have accumulated wealth. Many people who have failed to save for retirement may, at least, have a home and the equity in it to cushion their retirement.

If wealthy investors keep buying up single family homes and trailer parks, it will make it even harder for people to find affordable housing. Home ownership—that significant aspect of the American Dream—will suffer a damaging blow. Once again, people will be thinking that "the system is rigged." And they will be right.

Finding Alternate Routes

In *The Richest Man in New Babylon*, the central character's first stroke of good fortune comes when his half-sister offers him a place to stay. "For a few nights," she tells him. He learns to appreciate the value of her offer. Starting small (a baby step), he begins paying her rent. And over time, he earns her trust and her respect. For this fictional character who has just been released from incarceration, rebuilding this relationship is an essential step in his effort to grow and succeed in other aspects of his life.

When a low- or limited-income person sits down to develop a spending plan on paper, the expense for shelter is typically the biggest and most forbidding number they face. Looking at the initial cost for renting even the smallest apartment (at least two months' rent in advance, plus a security deposit) is incredibly discouraging. For people who are just starting out or starting over, finding an affordable place to live is a crucial first step.

For most of human history, multiple generations of families have lived in the same house. Is that a possibility? The typical American home today is not necessarily designed for multi-generation living, but perhaps, with good will all around, accommodations can be made?

Various types of communal living arrangements may provide shelter in the short term that can provide savings for the future. In post-WWII New York, artists took the lead in finding low-cost industrial space and converting it into highly desirable loft living. Creative, energetic people can seek out those kinds of opportunities in places where convertible buildings still exist.

In California, recently relaxed zoning laws have led to the creation of *granny flats*—small dwellings on the same property as an existing home. This change allows a garage, for example, to be improved to be a residence. It allows people with the right skills to apply them and build something like a contemporary log cabin.

Creative architects and others have started a tiny home movement.

People in areas with waterfronts frequently live on boats.

Mobile homes, though threatened, remain one of the nation's largest sources of affordable housing.

One effect of the Covid pandemic has been the great increase in workplace flexibility. If your office is wherever you find your Internet connection, that changes your geographic limits and may open up less expensive living locations to you. The unintended consequence of this, however, is rising home prices and affordability issues in popular locations where remote-capable workers are relocating.

Communal living, formal or informal, may provide refuge for some people.

Here is the heart of the matter. People cannot save money if they are forced to spend too much of their money on shelter. The shortest, most direct route to reducing the cost of shelter is the pooling of resources— living with extended family, friends, or trustworthy others and sharing expenses.

Shelter—payment for rent, mortgage, and property taxes—is typically going to be the biggest item on anyone's spending plan. If you can get that part right, you can position yourself to get on the road to financial serenity.

Follow the rules. Yes, follow Rule No. 1, for sure. But additionally, look for ways to spend less so you can save more. For young adults, especially, the idea of "living at home" may seem terrible. Parents may hate the idea just as much. But if you can put a year or two's worth of rent into savings (while paying your way at home, too), then the benefits can be significant.

Everyone needs shelter. When everyone needs something, it becomes a profitable business opportunity. The "shelter industry" in the United States is becoming an extension of the financial services industry that puts profits ahead of any other interests. It is time to recognize this kind of investment business as a predator, an adversary like credit card companies or the tobacco industry.

Think creatively. Follow *The Rules*. Fight back.

Appendix I

Cryptocurrency and NFTs

Bitcoin, other cryptocurrencies, cryptocurrency exchanges, and NFTs are in the news, flying high in social media and causing acute cases of FOMO (Fear of Missing Out). Get real, people!

The primary practical use of Bitcoin since it was conceived in 2009 has been to make untraceable payoffs to criminals and pay ransoms to computer hijackers. Small groups of early investors in currencies and exchanges have made a lot of real (actual government-backed) money. Later investors have not been as fortunate.

People who invest in crypto products today are unlikely to make large profits and may lose their investment entirely. Economists have described cryptocurrencies as a kind of Ponzi scheme—a type of financial fraud where the perpetrators use money from new investors to pay off early investors. This works until the whole scheme collapses of its own weight.

Celebrities and "influencers" who promote cryptocurrencies are being paid in some way—possibly in the cryptocurrency (which they immediately sell) or possibly in real money. They are not interested in your personal finances, nor do they have any responsibility to you. They have no special financial expertise. They are simply looking for ways to make more money for themselves.

Politicians who talk about cryptocurrency and even take some of their salaries in crypto cash are simply trying to look hip.

All of these kinds of currencies and businesses are, by definition, surrounded by secrecy and anonymity. They exist in a theoretical realm controlled by complex rules and mathematics (blockchain). The process for "mining" cryptocurrencies is environmentally destructive. It relies on vast arrays of computers, many powered by fossil fuel–generated electricity, that ultimately put more carbon dioxide into the atmosphere and increase global warming.

NFTs (non-fungible tokens) are similar to cryptocurrencies in that their ownership is recorded in a complex kind of mathematical convention (blockchain) that is a substitute for physical reality. They are generally easier to understand. They are similar to trading cards and other collectibles. In that respect, it is also easy to understand that, while they might increase in value, they may also lose value. They might become worthless. And they exist in an electronic environment where, if you lose your password or perhaps your computer crashes, you may lose your investment.

NFTs are believed to be used in money laundering operations. They are also subject to *rug pull* scams, where a developer promotes a project and then suddenly sells all the developer shares, takes the money, and disappears, destroying the value of the project. Rug pulls have become an increasingly common hazard when buying NFTs, with the proceeds of some rug pulls being valued at hundreds of thousands or even millions of dollars. Rug pulls accounted for 37 percent of all crypto-related scam revenue in 2021, according to one analysis.

Summary

If you have money for gambling and want to get into the crypto game or play with NFTs, you have lots of options. Maybe you'll be lucky, but be prepared to lose it all.

Appendix J
Savings and Retirement

Start saving for your retirement.
Start saving for your retirement.
Start saving for your retirement.

That's what they all say. Why?

Through the 1950s, the ideal future for older people in the United States was to retire with a pension. You worked hard, you contributed to the plan, and when you were eligible to retire, you would collect a pension sufficient to live on for the rest of your life.

Why can't you have a pension now?

That's easy. Because the presidents and CEOs of big companies don't need pensions. And if they don't need a pension, why should you?

In the 1950s, top executives at large corporations earned about 20 times as much as an average worker at the same company. The company's top executives relied on the same pension plan as the rest of the company's employees.

Today, corporate executives earn at least 70 times more than the average employee. At some companies, the top executives are paid factors of 100, 200, 300, or more times as much as an average employee.

If the CEOs and other executives needed a pension plan, the companies would make that a priority, and the company would have one. Since the executives earn so much money that they don't need pensions, they operate their businesses as though their employees shouldn't need pensions either.

Instead of pensions, employees typically are rewarded with a 401(k) plan so they can save for their own retirement just like their bosses do. And to show that the company cares, it may (though it isn't required) match a small percentage of the employee's contribution. It is also worth noting that the most highly compensated employees at a company get the greatest benefit from a 401(k) plan. They have the most money to contribute to it and can reasonably be expected to have the highest tax rates—therefore receiving the biggest tax benefit.

All of this works out well for company executives and wealthy company shareholders. A pension plan represents an expense. Employees are an expense. Minimizing expenses increases profitability. Corporate executives today are principally concerned with increasing profitability and adding shareholder value. This is generally referred to as having management *aligned* with shareholder interests.

There are a few places where pensions still exist—primarily in organizations where there are labor unions—but they are under assault by politicians. If you have the opportunity to work at an organization that offers a pension, it may prove to be a huge benefit to you in your retirement. It is not, however, something that you ought to take for granted. Many political and business interests are aligned to oppose the idea that American workers should have pensions. Where pension plans currently exist, they can and may be legally dissolved in the future.

Looking Ahead

Assuming that you are not going to have a pension, how much do you need to save for retirement? The rule of thumb changes over time. In 2022, the consensus seems to be 25 times the amount of income you hope to have after your retirement. Financial planning experts say this will allow you to withdraw about 4 percent of your savings annually, even if you live to a reasonably old age, without running out of money.

If you are qualified to receive Social Security benefits, financial planners will tell you that you can reduce your retirement income goal by the amount of Social Security income you expect to receive.

Following is a very simple chart that will give you a rough idea of how much money you ought to have in savings in order to have the income you expect after retirement.

Retirement: Expectations and Reality

Expected Annual Income	$25,000	$60,000	$100,000
Social Security*	$12,000	$30,000	$36,000
Shortfall	$13,000	$30,000	$74,000
Savings Goal	$325,000	$750,000	$1,850,000

Expected Annual Income: How much income do you think you will need when you retire?

Social Security: Social Security benefits can vary greatly. If someone takes the benefit early, the amount is reduced. If a person waits until age 70, the amount is increased. Variations in income over a person's working life change the benefit amount. These are ballpark estimates. Also remember, if you are counting on Social Security benefits from two people and one of the people dies, that benefit will be lost. A survivor benefit adjustment may be available, but a surviving spouse or partner will not continue to receive the same amount.

Shortfall: Subtract you Social Security income from the amount you think you will need to retire. If you have other sources of income from annuities, rental income, part-time work or some other sources you could subtract them too. The shortfall is an amount of annual income you will need to add in order to reach your Expected annual Income.

Savings Goal: Some professional financial planners recommend you have 25 times the amount of money you want to have in retirement income in order to retire without fear of the money running out. Here, for each scenario, is the amount of money a person would need to have saved to achieve their retirement income goal.

The one big additional asset many people will count on as retirement savings is their home equity. Unfortunately, many people who have reached retirement age still have mortgages. Even if you liquidate that asset, you are going to have to pay for shelter.

Professional financial planners and people in the financial services industry will identify sophisticated options for homeowners. There is something called a reverse mortgage, for example, which allows someone to (kind of) sell their house while still living in it. But, remember Rule No. 7 when you think about programs like that: The financial services industry always comes out ahead.

Retirement: Reality Check

Age Group	20-29	30-39	40-49	50-59	60-69
Amount in 401(k) Savings	$10,500	$38,400	$93,400	$160,000	$182,000

Here are the average 401(k) balances held by Americans by age group. Note that a 401(k) balance is only an *indicator* of the amount people have saved. They *may* have individual IRAs, Roth IRAs, stocks, CDs, and other savings. Total savings numbers, however, suggest that the 401(k) numbers are a reasonably accurate reflection of their financial reality.

Summary

Start saving for your retirement now!

Start when you are young, and the money you invest will have time to grow. Keep saving for retirement as you age. Use the maximum contribution rules as incentives to fill your retirement bucket. Become a savings fanatic as you approach retirement, when you hope to have fewer expenses (maybe you've paid off your mortgage) and you are earning more money.

Save. Save. Save. The worst thing that can happen is that you'll have too much money. Dang.

Appendix K

Credit Unions versus Banks

Everyone needs to be "banked." You **need** access to state-of-the-art online banking services with no-fee automated teller machines (ATMs), savings accounts, and checking accounts—and you need to get all of this at a fair price.

Before you open a bank account at the nearest commercial bank, you owe it to yourself to consider all your banking options—especially this one: bank or credit union?

Credit unions are nonprofit organizations created to serve their members. In order to use a credit union, you have to be a member. Sometimes, that means you have to be an employee at a specific company or a relative of an employee. But credit unions can have other membership criteria, such as where you live or membership in some other organization.

For one of the biggest credit unions, Consumers Credit Union, you are required to join the Consumers Cooperative Association (for a one-time, five-dollar fee). That qualifies you to become a member and join the Consumers Credit Union. Or, consider the nation's biggest credit union. Anyone who is serving or has served in any U.S. military branch or worked for the federal government (or is a relative of any of those people) is eligible to belong to the Navy Federal Credit Union.

A large, modern credit union (CU) offers all the same services as large banks. The overall costs for a credit union are lower. The major disadvantage of credit unions is that they typically have fewer in-person branches. To make up for that, large CUs have very large networks of fee-free ATMs, and they cooperate with other CUs to provide in-person "shared branch" services.

Banks are for-profit businesses. They have a responsibility to provide a financial return to their shareholders. As a result, they may have higher fees for some services, higher interest rates for loans, higher minimum deposit requirements, and higher charges for processing checks. Overall, they are usually more expensive than a comparable credit union.

The big advantage of banks is they have lots of branches where you can speak to someone in person.

Do your research. Look up credit unions and banks online. Personally, I have been a very satisfied credit union member for more than forty years. But, I have also worked with banks—specifically for mortgages and high interest-earning, online savings accounts.

The financial services industry in the United States is huge and highly profitable. Be a smart consumer (a cheapskate) and explore all your options when it's time to "get banked."

Appendix L
Can You Trust the Stock Market?

Why should anyone have confidence in the stock market? Here is a personal response to the question.

The American economy revolves around the stock market. Saving is not rewarded. The entire economic system is designed to encourage individuals to be investors.

Financial reporters frequently use the terms "bears" and "bulls" to describe investors. A bear is someone who thinks the market may go down. A bear is conservative. A bear wants to put money in a nice safe savings account.

Bulls are optimistic. They think stock prices will go up. They will probably reinvest any earnings from their stocks to buy more stocks.

Me? I'm not sure. I am ambivalent. Maybe I'm an imaginary creature—an ambullabear. (Or am I ambearabull?)

A Bear's Perspective

Seriously, how can you trust the stock market with your money? What about the market collapse in 2000? The housing market bubble in 2008? The market crash in 1929 that led to the Great Depression? The stock market can be a very scary place.

The current valuation of stocks seems too high to me. If you multiply the value of a stock times the number of outstanding shares, you get a number called the market capitalization (market cap). When you do the math for a lot of companies, the value that the market has given them seems far too high to me. Is Apple really worth $2.5 trillion? If you broke the company down and sold off the parts, could it be worth all that much money? I don't know, and I'm not qualified to have a professional opinion. But I am allowed to have gut feelings about this sort of thing.

Apple may be a bad example. It has huge revenues and an array of popular products and services. But many smaller companies seem to me to have very high valuations in comparison to the actual assets they have and the income they produce. And due to modern management practices, they have very low cash reserves, and they may have a great deal of debt.

During the 2008 financial crisis, there was talk about allowing major U.S. car manufacturers to go bankrupt. When financial experts considered that possible outcome, they said the car companies might have been worth 10 percent of their previous market cap, and maybe even less, if they were sold off in bankruptcy.

In recent years professional investors—in particular a group known as "activist" investors—have demanded that companies get rid of their cash reserves, sell off "underperforming" assets, and increase their debt. These actions have increased the value of the target companies in the stock market. But in my view (definitely that of a non-expert) they have hollowed out the companies, making them more vulnerable to failure.

So, there is a part of me that does not trust the stock market. Overall, it seems to keep doing better and better. How long can that go on? Is there a big collapse coming?

A Bull's Point of View

First, there is the historic record. Over time the American stock market has always delivered good results. Yes, there have been blips. But investors who buy and hold stocks—who "stay the course"—seem to always come out ahead in the long run.

And here's another, fairly cynical perspective on why someone should be a bull in thinking about the stock market.

Rich people have a lot of money invested in the stock market. The system is rigged to help them get richer. The people who run companies today are committed to increasing stock prices to help the rich people get richer. Government policy is guided by the interests of rich people.

With all of that in mind, it makes sense for us to invest in the stock market because we are lining ourselves up with the rich people. We can take advantage of the system they have set up to increase their own wealth. The odds are good that we will benefit. Our investments will grow. And beyond that, what other options are there?

My approach to the stock market today, especially if I were a young person, would be cautious and optimistic. I would listen to financial advisors that I trust and invest in stocks. I would listen to Warren Buffet and put money in a Vanguard S&P 500 index fund.

But Trust Your Gut

But—a big "but" here—I would be prepared to move my money out of stocks if I felt the market was facing a huge downturn like the tech stock bubble (2000) or the housing bubble (2008). Conventional wisdom says that "you can't time the market" and you should "ride out" downturns. So that was what I did over the years, and I regret it.

There are times when someone with no special expertise can see that the stock market is taking a big tumble. In that kind of situation, a non-expert might think it would be a good idea to pull their money out of stocks. Perhaps it would be a good time to log into their 401(k) (or other investment) account and move their funds into a safe haven like a money market account or a savings account.

My thought is this. If you have a gut instinct that you should take action, trust your gut. You may forego a little bit of profit when the stock market comes back (as it always seems to do) but you will have taken control over your investments and maybe learned a thing or two along the way.

When the market takes a big slide, do you think all the very rich people with their expertise and financial advisors are just going to "stay the course" and watch the value of their portfolios plummet?

I don't think so. I think they take action. So I think it's okay for us to take action, too.

Part IV
Glossary

Glossary

glos·sa·ry

/ˈglôsəre/

plural noun: appendices

1. an alphabetical listing of words, terms, acronyms, and phrases used in or related to a specific subject

More Boring Stuff

WARNING: Boring Stuff. But this is all terminology you need to understand so that people—especially people selling financial services—can't baffle you with their Boring Stuff. This list is not comprehensive. It is **NOT** everything you might need to know. But it's a good start.

A Few Words of Wisdom

Neither a borrower nor a lender be,
For loan oft loses both itself and friend,
And borrowing dulls the edge of husbandry.

William Shakespeare
Hamlet Act I, scene 3

Annual income twenty pounds, annual expenditure nineteen and six, result happiness. Annual income twenty pounds, annual expenditure twenty pounds ought and six, result misery.

Charles Dickens,
David Copperfield

I love money. I love everything about it. I bought some pretty good stuff. Got me a $300 pair of socks. Got a fur sink. An electric dog polisher. A gasoline powered turtleneck sweater. And, of course, I bought some dumb stuff, too.

Steve Martin

My grandpa used to tell my dad,
"Son, it's not the money you make,
it's the money you hold on to."

Austin Kleon
Steal Like an Artist

A journey of a thousand miles must begin with a single step.

Lao Tzu

Glossary

401(k) plan

The name—401(k) plan—comes from a section of the U.S. Tax Code. A 401(k) plan may be offered by a for-profit company. Similar 403(b) plans may be offered by a nonprofit organization. These "tax-advantaged" plans are designed for retirement savings and retirement savings only. The tax advantage they offer is that you do not have to pay income taxes on money before it goes into the plan. You will, however, have to pay taxes on the money when, after you reach retirement age, you withdraw money. Theoretically, you will be earning less money and your tax rate will be lower. However, you hope your investments will have grown and you will pay taxes on all of it upon withdrawal.

Organizations offering 401(k) and 403(b) plans *may* offer to match your contributions to the plan. Your contributions are based on your pay. You might, for example, contribute 2 percent of your pay to the plan. An employer might match that. Some employers might offer to match a higher contribution. Generally, financial advisors recommend contributing at least as much to this kind of retirement plan as employers are willing to match. Otherwise, they will say you are leaving money on the table.

If you withdraw money from one of these plans before you reach the designated age, you will have to pay a penalty unless the withdrawal is for a hardship exemption such as a medical emergency or home-buying expense for a primary residence. Even if you do not have to pay a penalty, you do have to pay income tax on your withdrawal.

These kinds of plans are an inexpensive (to the employer) substitute for the kind of defined pension plans that businesses offered through the middle of the 20th century. The only places where pensions have survived to any great extent are in government service and in workplaces with strong unions. Even there, they are under attack. The U.S. economic system is not designed to make it easy for people to retire.

Account Number

When applying Rule No. 6 (Make It Automatic) you will likely find times when you will need to know your credit union or bank account number. This can be tricky. You may have a customer ID number that is not the same as your account number, and you will have separate account numbers for your checking, savings, and other accounts. When you set up direct deposit for your pay, you may be asked to provide a voided check. That will give your employer's payroll processor your bank checking account number. That's where your pay will be deposited.

Advertising

(see Marketing)

APR

Annual Percentage Rate. Banks, stores, and credit card issuers all compete by advertising goods, loans, and credit card balance charges with low APR. When you follow Rule No. 4 and Never Pay Interest, you don't care what anybody's APR is. If you still have some debt, pay attention to the APR for the debt you have, and take that into consideration while you work to eliminate it. You may want to pay the debts with the highest APR first.

Asset

Anything you own that has value. Typically, when you consider your assets you value them at their market price. If you sell the asset, how much will someone pay for it? The cash assets in your bank account will hold 100 percent of their value. However, if you think of a vehicle, a diamond necklace, or a rare pair of Air Jordans as an asset, you would have to ask, realistically, how much can I get if I sell this?

ATM

Automated Teller Machine. Once upon a time we went into a bank and met human beings called "tellers" to deposit paychecks and withdraw money. Not so much anymore. When you shop for financial services—

specifically when choosing between a bank or a credit union—the availability of ATMs can be an important consideration. Credit unions typically have fewer physical locations (branches) than commercial banks. They try to make up for that by having a large network of no-fee ATMs available for their customers. Credit unions also offer shared service locations with other credit unions, so you can often get the same kind of in-person service, even if it is a different organization. ATMs are the public face of the modern baking system around the world. When working with ATMs, your goal is to never pay fees in the U.S. and to pay the lowest possible fees and currency exchange rates when out of the country. Do your homework!

Autopay
Online transactions often include an option to "autopay" or "auto-renew." Frequently, avoiding an autopay requires you to find a small checkbox somewhere on the screen. The vendors require you to opt out. And in some instances, the online vendor requires you to use an autopay plan. They say you can opt out later. Beware of autopay. If the site enrolls you automatically, contact it right away and say you want to opt out now. You may forget to cancel it later. Check your credit card statements carefully. A $5 monthly renewal fee for a service you aren't using will add up (drip, drip, drip).

Bankruptcy
Bankruptcy allows a debtor to "discharge" (eliminate) some types of debt. Credit card debt, personal loans, and bills for some service providers, for example, could be written off. Bill collectors cannot try to collect for debt discharged in bankruptcy. In recent years, bankruptcy laws have been modified to make it more difficult to discharge debts. Taxes and criminal fines cannot be included in bankruptcy. Student loans are nearly impossible to include in bankruptcy. The new bankruptcy laws may require people who are filing for certain types of bankruptcy to work with credit counseling agencies (business-supported, nonprofit bill collection agencies). Bankruptcy requires the services of an attorney, and all fees must be paid in advance. If you think you are a candidate for bankruptcy, you can meet with a bankruptcy attorney. It can be very informative. Most bankruptcy attorneys will offer one free meeting with potential new clients.

Banks, Savings Banks, Savings and Loans
All are part of the commercial banking industry. They are profit-making businesses and are operated with an eye toward rewarding their managers, owners, and investors. In the past many small banks served central roles in cities and towns, earning income by investing depositors' money into loans to local businesses and mortgages for local homeowners. Individuals frequently had personal relationships with bank executives.

Today, regional and national banks dominate the commercial banking industry. They sell a vast array of products and services. It is an increasingly automated, impersonal kind of business for ordinary consumers. Still, having a good banking relationship is important—even if it is through a smartphone or computer. It is a good idea to periodically assess the services your bank provides and, especially if you have to pay any fees, shop around for a better financial service provider.

Branding
(Catchy term for advertising. See Marketing.)

Budget, Budgeting
For individuals and families, this is a traditional exercise in which people make a careful list of all their expenses and income and see if they have enough money to live on. The budget creators then make enough adjustments to assure themselves that they will be able to make it through to the next pay period. Then, usually, the budget is put away and ignored until the next financial crunch, when they prepare another budget. The whole idea of a budget is negative. Use the term "spending plan." Please see the entry under Spending Plan.

Celebrating Success

It is very important to reward yourself for doing good work. Remember: It is work! It is hard! When you reach a goal or pass a milestone, you need to give yourself credit. Even better, share it. Friends, loved ones, members of your support team—let them know. Get together with some of them. The home team has scored a victory. Celebrate it. (See the glossary entry on Keeping Score.)

Credit Card

A credit card allows the cardholder to spend (borrow) money up to the card's credit limit. At the end of the card's monthly billing cycle, the cardholder receives a statement and bill. The cardholder can pay the bill in full and is required to make at least a minimum payment.

Credit cards are the ultimate good/evil combination. Evil credit cards provide an easy way to spend more money than you have, get into debt, and find yourself in deep financial trouble. If you don't pay off your balance in full, the credit card issuer can charge a huge amount of interest (15, 20, 30 percent or more; there's no legal limit). If you miss a payment, the credit card issuer charges a fee. Fail to pay off the card in full again, and you'll pay interest on the outstanding balance and the fee.

Credit cards are good when the monthly statement is paid in full, on time, every time. They provide convenience and rewards (such as up to 5 percent cash back). Remember Rule No. 4, Never Pay Interest, and you will always have a good credit card. If you break Rule No. 4 with a credit card, you should lock up or cut up your evil credit card.

Certificate of Deposit (CD)

Banks and credit unions offer certificates of deposit (CDs). CDs offer savers a higher interest rate than ordinary savings accounts or money market accounts. CDs offer a fixed interest rate for a specific term. For example, you might get 1 percent interest for a one-year CD but 1.5 percent interest for a five-year CD. Certificates of deposit offer savers a little more interest, but they can be easily transferred back into a checking or savings account if the saver needs access to the funds. If you "cash in" a CD before it "matures" (reaches the end of the time you agreed to hold it when you purchased it) you may forfeit a few months' worth of interest or more. Read the fine print.

Certifications

Community colleges and for-profit schools offer a wide range of certificates that are designed to prepare students for job opportunities. Many are well respected and professionally useful. Unfortunately, some are not. It's important for students to be aware that obtaining certification does not assure the student of getting a job. Many employers believe that actual work experience in a field is much more important than certification. Before committing to a certification program, the student should ask lots of questions about the program, look online to see if there have been any complaints, and ask to speak to students who have gotten jobs. Education is an investment of your time and money. Do your research and invest wisely.

CFPB

The Consumer Financial Protection Bureau (CFPB) is a good source of information about your rights in financial disputes, debt collection, credit reports, and any other matters related to loans and finance. The CFPB's services overlap, to some extent, with the Federal Trade Commission (FTC). Check the websites for both organizations for information when you have questions related to credit reports, debt collection, other personal financial issues, and your rights.

Charge-Off

This term is used by credit bureaus for a bill that a consumer does not pay in full. If, for example, a person fails to pay a credit card balance, the card is deactivated. The credit card company then starts collection proceedings. If the company decides that the bill is uncollectable, typically after about six months, the debt can become a charge-off. The company reports this to the credit bureaus and it will remain on the person's credit report for seven years. A charge-off has a serious negative impact on the person's credit report and credit score, but it will not have any legal impact unless some kind of fraud was involved. Even if the company that originally incurred the debt decides not to pursue collection, it may sell the uncollected bill to another company that specializes in debt collection. Despite the charge-off, the person with the debt may face another round of collection proceedings.

Cheapskate

Some people think that being a cheapskate is a bad thing. They are wrong. Being responsible and keeping the money that you earn is a good thing to do. Don't let someone else's label influence how much you spend.

Coach, Coaching

People who play sports have coaches who help them get better at their games. The same thing can be true with your personal finances. You can pay professional financial advisors to help you manage money more effectively. There are also free online resources available. You can turn to elders or even peers that you trust to discuss finances, develop strategies and motivate you. Yes, It's All up to You (Rule No. 10), but you don't have to do it alone.

Compounding, Compound Interest

When you put your money in a savings account, it earns interest. Then the interest is added to your savings (the principal). The next time the interest is calculated, it is based on the new, larger number. Your savings are compounded. That's all good. Old books about personal finance refer to this as "the magic" of compound interest.

If you owe money, like the balance on a credit card, the same kind of compounding occurs. The amount you owe is added to your debt. In the next billing cycle, the new interest amount you owe is based on that larger total and your debt grows even faster. You can think of that as "the evil" of compounding.

Consumerism

Consumerism is the desire of people to consume more, buy more, and own more stuff. Consumerism is fueled by profit-seeking businesses. Remember this—imprint it on your brain in big, glowing letters—everyone wants you to give them your money. If you turn on a television, listen to the radio, look at a computer, walk down a busy street, open your mail, look at a magazine, go to an entertainment event, or even spend time sitting in a waiting room—do just about anything—you will be bombarded with images and messages designed to make you want stuff and give other people your money. And if you do get the stuff they are selling, you'll get more messages and more encouragement to get more stuff. It never ends. In America today it is essential to armor yourself against all the messages urging you to spend more so you can consume more. They all want your money. Don't give it to them.

Cooking

Cooking might seem unrelated to personal financial management, but it's not. Managing money is stressful. If you want to be successful, you need maintain your health. Good nutrition through a proper diet is essential. For many people—perhaps even most men—cooking is something they expect someone else to do. Thinking that way is a mistake. It is an especially big financial mistake if it results a diet of junk food, fast food, and other edible food-like substances.

Think about it. Learning to be a good cook helps your spend less money (Rule No. 2) and develop new skills (Rule No. 5). A better diet and understanding of nutrition can lead to good changes (Rule No. 8). And you can save more money (Rule No. 1) while taking more responsibility for an essential aspect of your life (Rule No. 10). Measure your ingredients carefully. Follow *The Rules*. Cook up a rich, nourishing financial future.

Credit Bureau, Credit Report, Credit Score
See Appendix C, where these terms are defined and put in context.

Credit Card
A credit card is a wallet-sized plastic card that has a magnetic strip and usually a microchip. It allows the cardholder to take out small loans to buy stuff. If the cardholder fails to pay the balance of the loans taken out with the card in full when a monthly statement says the balance is due, the cardholder is charged interest. If the cardholder is late in making a payment or fails to make a payment, the cardholder must pay a penalty fee. If you live by Rule No. 4, you always pay credit card statement balances in full. If you don't have enough money to do that, you are living beyond your means.

Credit Counseling
The credit counseling industry was established in the 1950s. Banks, credit card companies, and lenders were concerned about bankruptcies and write-offs. They got behind an effort to create "non-profit" agencies that would work with customers to help them arrange payments. In other words—a network of industry-sponsored bill collectors. Today the industry has grown extensively. The claim that some of these companies are not for-profit is undermined by the fact that the management and employees of these businesses are very well compensated. Credit counseling today includes nonprofit and for-profit businesses. Some of them say they do not charge fees, although they are compensated is other ways. Some do charge fees. These businesses are (very) loosely regulated by the FTC.

If you are thinking about working with a credit counseling business, consider the following facts. They are debt collection businesses. They have no fiduciary responsibility to you; they are not committed to serving your best financial interest. (See the glossary entry on Fiduciary.) Their business requires them to get you to pay as much as they can. Anything they say they will do for you is something you can do for yourself. If you want to pay for someone to do this work for you, make every effort to find out exactly how much it is going to cost you. Any extra costs are a kind of interest that, per Rule No. 4, you do not want to pay.

Credit Freeze
Anyone is allowed to place a credit freeze on their credit report. This restricts access to the credit report. Neither you nor anyone else will be able to open a credit card or loan account with a credit freeze in place. You can temporarily remove the freeze if you want to apply for credit. Even while the freeze is in effect, you will be able to do other things that may require access to your credit history, such as rent an apartment or apply for a job. There is no fee for setting up a credit freeze. You must contact each of the three major credit bureaus separately.

Credit Union
A nonprofit financial institution that is owned by its members. Large, well-managed credit unions today provide the same or better services than for-profit banks, in many cases with lower fees and higher interest rates for savings. When looking for a financial services provider, credit unions deserve strong consideration alongside banks.

Deadbeat
If you stop communicating with a company you owe money to or a collection agency representing a company you owe money to, you become a "deadbeat." As the word suggests, you become a kind of nonperson and lose any goodwill you might have had and may forgo a possible settlement for the debt. This book's recommendation: Don't be a deadbeat. Stay in communication. Even if you cannot pay anything now, you can keep your future options open.

Debt
The money you owe. Dangerous stuff. Avoid it whenever possible.

The Rules

Debit Card

A debit card is sort of like a credit card, but different in some key ways. When you use a debit card, money is immediately withdrawn from the bank account that it is linked to. You typically have to provide a personal identification number (PIN). The transaction fees charged to a merchant are lower for a debit card than for a credit card, so merchants prefer them. Theoretically, if you don't have enough money in the account, the charge will be declined. Theoretically, you should not be able to go into debt when using a debit card.

In reality, some financial institutions that offer debit cards honor transactions that exceed your account balance. Then they charge you a fee or a penalty, and you end up in debt, just as you might with a credit card. So, if you have a debit card, be sure to read the fine print, and, more practically, talk to the people who issue the card and ask them about these kinds of situations. "What happens if . . . ?" If you are a person who wants to follow *The Rules*, it's preferable to have a charge declined than to be hit with an unexpected fee or penalty.

Debt Consolidation (Simplifying Your Life)

Be careful. Be very careful. The biggest beneficiaries of debt consolidation loans are the financial service providers and the companies holding the debt.

People who promote debt consolidation loans (and this includes student loan refinancing) make big promises. They tell you they are "simplifying your life." You'll have fewer bills to pay. And you'll have lower payments, too. What could be better?

What is better is really simplifying your life by getting rid of those debts. Yes, it may mean making real sacrifices. It may mean making do with less—a lot less. But when you refinance (and consolidate) debt, you end up paying more money and living with the burden longer. You are making things better for lenders who are profiting from your uncomfortable situation.

And there is one more thing to fear—in particular with student loan refinancing. You may be giving up some important benefits including possible student loan forgiveness. Refinancing a federal student loan, for example, may involve trading off forgiveness of the loan 20 years after it was issued to slightly lower payments forever. "Simplify your life" is marketing jargon for "pay us more money and we'll send you a smaller bill for a lot longer." Real simplifying is getting rid of your debts and not adding any new ones.

Deductible

An insurance industry term applicable to automotive, home, medical, and other insurance policies. The deductible is the amount of money you have to pay before your insurance coverage goes into effect. Typically, the lower the deductible, the higher the cost of the insurance (premium).

Direct Deposit

Direct deposit allows your employer to deposit your pay directly in your bank or credit union account. No check cashing, no money in hand, no risk of spending a little extra because you've got a lot of cash. Direct deposit is good. If you can get it, use it.

Diversification

Don't put all your eggs in one basket. Don't put all your money in one investment option. Typically you hear about diversification when you're asked to choose the investments for your 401(k) or similar investment plan. You'll be offered an array of stock funds, bond funds, maybe some real estate funds, and probably a money market account. Advisors, rightly, tell you to put some money in several different funds.

Some companies offer their own company stock as an investment option, and they may actively encourage employees to invest their money in it. You probably do not want to put all your money in your company's stock (look up Enron.) And if you leave the company and have a significant amount of company stock, you may want to seek professional advice on how to manage it.

Do the Math
This is shorthand for "multiply any little expenses by the number of times in a day or a week you incur them, and then figure out how much they cost you over the course of an entire year." If it turns out to be a big number, maybe cut down on that "little" expense. If it's a really big number, maybe it will motivate you to quit.

Drip Saving
Save your pocket change in a jar. At the end of a year, you'll be surprised. Put half of it in your savings and spend the other half on a nice dinner to reward yourself for being a saver.

DRIP Investing
A Dividend Reinvestment Plan (DRIP) is an investment option that allows you to invest a small amount of money into a specific stock that typically pays dividends. DRIP investing allows you to put a little bit of money into an account every month and perhaps only buy a small percentage of a share of a stock. You continue to add money to buy more of the stock and, when it issues dividends, your profit is used to buy more of the stock.

In the past, DRIP plans had other advantages over individual stock brokerage accounts (no brokerage fees, ability to buy partial shares), but regular brokerages offer those benefits now. Still, a DRIP is a relatively simple approach to hands-off investing for the long term. There is a list of "dividend aristocrats" that you can look up that are good candidates for DRIP investing. And some companies, like Coca-Cola and Johnson & Johnson, operate their own DRIP plans.

Drip Spending
A little expense every day that can add up. It's like a dripping faucet. Leave it alone, and you may soon have a flooded basement.

Emergency Fund
In is essential to have money set aside in case of emergencies. There is no such thing as an unexpected emergency. You know you will have unplanned expenses that come up suddenly—you just don't know what they will be.

Read Appendix A, The Emergency Savings Fund Crisis, carefully. Remember Rule No. 1. Take action and take control of your financial future.

Envelope System
A spending plan (budget) system designed for people who prefer to do all their personal financial business in cash. People using the envelope system maintain a set of labeled envelopes: rent, groceries, electric, telephone, etc. They put cash in the envelopes and use the money in each envelope to pay the appropriate bill. This is not a system that we recommend (see Rule No. 6) but it works well for some people. They swear by it. Remember, the most important thing in personal financial management is to find a system that works for you and then stick with it.

Equity
Equity is a word used in two ways. In discussing things that you are purchasing with a loan, it refers to the amount of the thing that you are buying that you actually own. If you have paid down half of a home mortgage, for example, your equity would be half of the appraised value of the property. The word equity is also used by stock brokers and other investment advisors to refer to stocks, bonds, and shares of investment funds. The financial profession refers to them as equities.

Escrow
An escrow account is a bank account where money is set aside for a special purpose. Frequently mortgage service companies will require homeowners to pay into an escrow account that is used to pay for the property's insurance and taxes. The

escrow account protects the mortgage holder from losses that might occur if the homeowner failed to make these payments. When a mortgage is paid off in full, the homeowner takes over responsibility for these payments.

Estate or Inheritance Taxes

Money you inherit is not usually considered taxable income. Estate taxes are something that very rich people think about. They pay lobbyists to fight against them tooth and nail. If you have assets of more than $10 million, you might be affected by an inheritance tax. If you have assets worth more than $10 million, you have accountants and tax advisors to help you answer any questions.

Executor

When you create a will, you must identify an executor, someone who will help see that your last wishes are fulfilled and deal with the remaining details related to your estate. Typically, it will be someone who is younger and who knows you and your family. Creating your will is a way to focus your attention on this matter. Whomever you select, do *not* let it be a surprise for them after the fact. Talk to them, be sure it's okay with them, and talk about your will. Make life easy for the people you care about, even if you're not around.

Exercise

Getting in shape financially can be stressful. It's hard work. Sometimes it demands sacrifice. You need to be in good physical shape to get the job done. Take care of your body. Exercise, eat healthy foods, and stay in shape. You're in this for the long haul, and you will enjoy life more if you are in the best physical shape you can be in. (Also see Nutrition.)

Faith

Some readers may say that they should put contributions to their religious faith ahead of even Rule No. 1. It is impossible to argue against that kind of commitment. Abiding faith can be a powerful motivator for dealing with personal financial issues. A religious community can be an important part of the "team" that assists you. Responsible, caring leaders and members of any faith-based group should fully support any member who wants to be sure they have an emergency fund and are starting to build a retirement fund, even if that reduces the contributions they can make to the religious community.

FDIC

The Federal Deposit Insurance Corporation guarantees your bank account up to $250,000. If your bank fails, you still get your money. The NCUA provides the same insurance for credit unions.

Fees

The little extra charges that you have to pay. You can find fees anywhere. Cable television bills, telephone bills, and mortgages frequently include fees. It is important for you to understand what the fees are for. Contact the companies and ask about them. There will be times you will find that you can make changes—buy a component instead of renting it or make some other modification—that will save you a recurring monthly fee. It is worth the effort to ask about any fee on a bill that you don't fully understand.

FICO

Fair, Isaac & Company (FICO) invented the "credit score." It has a major competitor, VantageScore, a company created by the three major credit bureaus. Read Appendix C for the information you need to know about credit scores.

Fiduciary

If someone is a fiduciary, they have agreed that they will make recommendations and act solely in your best interest and not their own. The law requires them to do what is best for you.

Most of the people you encounter in the financial services industry are not fiduciaries. They are not obligated to what is best for you. It is important to keep that in mind when working with financial professionals and trying to determine whom you can count on as a trusted advisor.

Financial Management Apps

Dozens (possibly hundreds) of smartphone and computer apps are available to assist people with money management. Some are free. Some may have a one-time cost. Some are sold by subscription. If you feel like you want to supplement your online banking access with additional financial management tools, there are lots and lots of choices. Some of these apps link to bank, credit union, mortgage, vehicle loan, 401(k) and other accounts. They read data from credit card transactions and break it out into spending categories, showing you where your money is going. If you are ambitious and adept, you may want to create your own spreadsheet or database to track your financials. You might even want to use a full-featured accounting program like Quicken. The capability of this type of technology is extraordinary, especially when you consider that only a few decades ago, people were still "crunching the numbers" with pen on paper, balancing their checkbooks.

Do research. Test out some candidates. Find a system that works for you. Use it to keep score.

Fixed Costs, Fixed Expenses

When you develop a spending plan, one of the things you need to include are your fixed costs (or fixed expenses). This is a bill that is the same every time it comes due. Fixed cost items include things like rent, most loan payments, and some utility bills. If money is tight in your spending plan, minimize the number of fixed cost items you have to deal with and, whenever possible, take control of them.

Some utility companies offer an averaging service for payments, calculating your typical annual expense and billing it in equal monthly amounts. This helps take an expense that can be quite variable and make it more like a fixed expense.

Flexible Spending Account (FSA)

A benefit offered by employers that is actually a pretty good deal. It allows you to pay for important services such as day care, commuting costs, and some medical expenses with pretax dollars. You don't have to pay income tax for that money—ever. It can result in dollars—not just pennies—in savings.

But FSAs are complicated. You have to decide in advance how much you want to spend. If you don't spend the money, you lose it. There are limits, too, and reporting requirements. FSAs are more valuable to wealthier (or at least higher-paid) employees (since they typically have higher tax rates). But for anyone who pays income taxes, an FSA can be a significant benefit—maybe hundreds of dollars a year. If your employer offers FSAs, get all the details and see how they might work for you.

For-Profit Schools

Most public schools, community colleges, four-year colleges, and universities are organized as not-for-profit businesses. Make no mistake—they are still businesses. They have budgets, and they must meet payroll and do everything necessary to keep their doors open—but they do not have to return a profit to their shareholders.

Meanwhile, thanks to money available to students in grants, and especially because of student loans, a lot of companies have expanded or gotten into the for-profit education business. They are accountable to shareholders and are motivated to bring in more money than they pay out for educating their students. They market aggressively and encourage students to take out student loans, even if their programs are unlikely to provide the students with great employment opportunities. For-profit schools have closed before students graduate, leaving them with no certification and deep in debt. And more than a few for-profit schools have been exposed as shams—promising a lot and delivering very little.

The Rules

Any time you sign up for a course with a for-profit educational business, you need to do extra research. Talk to graduates—lots of graduates. Be sure the business is delivering what it promises. The same warning applies to nonprofit educational institutions, too. But in general, they are less aggressive about their marketing, less pushy in getting people to sign up for their offerings, and not driven by a desire to return a profit.

Friction

When dealing with money, a little friction can be a good thing. If you make it a little harder to get cash or spend money on stuff, that little delay gives you time to think about what you're doing. It takes a day or two to transfer money from one online bank's high-interest savings account to an individual's personal online checking account. That extra time is a kind of friction that is a good thing for financial decision-making.

FTC

The Federal Trade Commission (FTC) provides accurate information for you about your rights as a "consumer" in the United States. You will find useful information about what bill collectors can and cannot do. You will also find information about credit reports (credit bureaus, credit scores, free credit reports, etc.) The FTC's services overlap to some extent with the Consumer Financial Protection Bureau (CFPB). Check the websites for both organizations when you have questions related to credit reports, debt collection, other financial issues, and your rights.

Full Disclosure

Any time you sign a financial agreement, you are supposed to get documentation that describes all the terms and conditions and "what ifs" and "gotchas." You can be sure that you will not read all the documents. You should, but you won't. You typically trust the people you are working with and hope you have some legal protection.

Here is one reasonable thing you can do. Ask questions. Ask the person or people you are dealing with "what happens if . . . " and "is it possible that . . ." and "if there is a problem, what do I . . ." Think about worst-case scenarios and ask about them. Listen to what the other folks say, for sure. But also listen to how they say it. How do you feel about what they are saying? If you are the slightest bit uncomfortable, maybe you should take the paperwork home and think about it some more. Reading that fine print is always a good idea.

Gift Card

Gift cards really suck. Okay, if it's a $10 card for a coffee shop around the corner from your office that the boss hands out on employee appreciation day, maybe it's okay—maybe. And maybe not even that.

Here are the problems with gift cards. (a) Recipients have to *spend* the money, typically, *at a place that has been preselected for them.* They don't have any option to apply Rule No. 1— and *SAVE MONEY!* (b) Gift cards get lost, or they get used but left with a balance, and then misplaced. This is all great news for the people who want to sell you stuff—they get free money. According to surveys, more than half of the people in the U.S. have unused gift cards, with an average balance of $115. That adds up to $15 billion—*unspent and unsaved.* A nice gift—*to the card-issuing businesses.* (c) Gift cards are lazy. I mean seriously, couldn't you take the time to think about the person and find an appropriate gift? Or alternately, if you want to let the person decide how to spend the money, can't you just give them cash or a check?

Gratitude

Think about the good things in your life. Write them down to make it more real. Some people do this daily and call it a *gratitude journal*. No matter where you're going and what obstacles you face, it's always a good time to think about the good people and good things in your life. Remember Rule No. 9.

Identity Theft
Don't give anyone your Social Security number unless there is a really, really good reason. Your employer. Your tax return. That should be about it. Identity theft is a big problem out in the real world. Scammers can set up accounts in your name, take out loans, run up bills, and leave you in big financial trouble. That's just in the real world. In the online world, it's worse. Much, much worse. And in the online world—when you get scammed, you have very little chance of getting your money back.

Identity theft is a big, real problem. Visit the FTC and CFPB websites, and read everything they have to say on the subject. That will be a good start for getting yourself educated about the problems you can face if you give personal information to the wrong people.

Inflation
An economist's term for higher prices. The overall cost of goods and services is measured by the government and reported as a percentage (the rate of inflation). If the rate of inflation is higher than the interest rate you are earning on your savings, experts say that you are losing money—you are losing "purchasing power."

In a market-based economy there are ways to address inflation. It's important for you to remember that you have choices. If the price goes up for something, you have an incentive to try alternatives. You may keep using something longer, opt for repairs, or look for a used (previously owned) substitute. Inflation is an important factor in the money game. But remember it's a game and you, as a consumer, have choices.

Interest
Interest is both money you receive when you loan money to someone and money you pay when you borrow money from someone. Rule No. 4 says you should minimize the money you pay out and maximize the money you receive. If you follow *The Rules*, you will earn much more money in interest than you pay in interest. You will pay little interest unless you have a mortgage.

Intestate
A term to describe a person who dies without a will.

IRA
An Individual Retirement Account (IRA) is a lot like a 401(k) plan, except there is no option for an employer to contribute to it. It is tax-advantaged. You put money in without paying taxes; you pay the tax when the money is withdrawn. The money is invested in funds that you get to choose. There's no extra tax on it while it is in the account. There is a tax penalty for early withdrawal unless there are special circumstances (one is medical expenses). You have to pay the taxes then, too. IRAs are a good way to save for retirement—nothing else.

Keeping Score
Managing money is hard work. It is stressful, and there are times when you just want to close your eyes and hope for the best. No! Don't do that. Find ways—at least one way—to keep score and track your success. You can't feel like you're winning if you don't know the score. One very basic place to start is your emergency savings fund. Set a goal. Then start working to achieve it. Start with a baby step (Rule No. 3). Keep score. Reach your goal. Now set a little higher goal (Rule No. 5). Keep at it and keep score. Track your success and build on it.

Liability
Liability is similar to debt, but trickier. Debt is money you owe now. A liability is money that you may owe now or that may become money you owe in the future.

Liquidity
Liquidity means this: How quickly can you use this money like cash? Savings and checking accounts are "liquid." You can write a check. You can go to an ATM and take out cash. When you put savings into a 401(k) plan, IRA, or similar investment, it is not liquid. It takes paperwork and a lot of time to turn money from one of these

accounts into cash in hand. Money "saved" in jewelry or gold coins represents an extremely nonliquid asset. It takes time, and you must find a buyer or broker to turn this kind of saving into cash—and you will likely lose a lot of the value of the asset in the process.

Your emergency fund needs to be kept as a liquid asset—a checking or a savings account, for example. You could put your emergency fund in a high-interest checking account in a separate institution that is linked to your regular bank account. That keeps your money liquid but provides just a little bit of "friction" to make you think before tapping into it.

Retirement funds are well kept in investment accounts, where it is not easy to take money out until you actually need it for retirement.

Living Expenses

How much does it cost you to live? This is like the "is the glass half full or half empty" question. When you are thinking about your spending plans, you can consider all the things you feel that you really need to live, come up with a price tag for them, and set that as your "living expense" number. Or, you can pick a number—a smaller number—say that's it, and stick to it. You'll have to scramble, make do, compromise on some things, and go without on others. In the end, you'll be surprised to find out that you didn't really need some things. And you'll be surprised at how much more of your hard-earned money you get to keep for yourself.

Living Will

A document you prepare to tell people what you want to happen in case you are incapacitated by illness or injury. Free online tools are available to do this. Yes, it's difficult. But you make decisions for yourself and take a great burden off the people closest to you. All documents like this must be properly signed with witnesses and notarized to be legally binding.

Marketing

This umbrella term includes advertising, branding, social influencing, promoting, enticing, and anything else designed to sell you "stuff" you don't need. Some effort goes into encouraging you to buy stuff from one supplier instead of another. Some is designed to get you to buy stuff you don't already have. Some try to get you to replace something you already have that is working fine with something they say works better. Learn to recognize this kind of influence peddling when you see or hear it. People in the marketing business are smart, do lots of research, and get paid the big bucks to influence you. Be aware that this is happening; fight back and resist. Make decisions about spending your hard-earned money slowly and carefully. Don't let marketing experts make decisions for you.

Meditation, Mindfulness

Money management can be highly stressful, especially when you feel like you don't have enough money. Finding a way to relax, step back, and think more clearly is valuable. Meditation (also called *mindfulness*) can do just that: help you clear your head and reduce the stress you feel. Community organizations may offer free classes. You can find numerous video tutorials available free on YouTube. Good money management requires clear thinking. Meditation can help.

Mentor

People with experience or skills that they are willing to share with you. A mentor is someone you respect who is willing to make time to meet with you and talk with you. A mentor could be a teacher or a coach, a close relative, an old friend, a supervisor at work, or someone you meet on a team, at a church, or through a friend. Here's one thing you need to remember about finding a mentor—they need to be the kind of person who can really help you become a better person and succeed in life. But—mentoring is a two-way process. In order for you to have a mentor, you've got to open yourself up and be ready to listen, take advice, try things out, and accept criticism. If you want to have a great teacher, you have to be a great student.

Money Market Account
A money market account is similar in most respects to a high-interest savings account. It's nearly as "liquid" as a checking account; it earns a tiny amount more in interest. Money market accounts available through online banking services provide you with some extra buckets where you can allocate your savings. Your emergency savings fund might be kept in a money market account, for example. Money market funds are not, however, FDIC or NCUA insured.

NCUA
The National Credit Union Association (NCUA) is a federal organization that provides the same deposit insurance for credit unions that the FDIC provides for banks. Credit union accounts are insured against any losses for up to $250,000. The NCUA insures deposits at federally regulated credit unions, protects the members who own credit unions, and charters and regulates federal credit unions.

Needs vs. Wants
There are lots of things we think we need that are really things we only want. Learn to tell the difference between them. It will save you a lot of money.

Net Worth
Add up all your assets. Then add up all your debts. Subtract your debts from your assets. If you have a positive number, that is your net worth. If it is a negative number, you are underwater. You owe more than you have. You could be said to have a "negative net worth."

Nutrition
You are what you eat. You need to know the difference between carbohydrates and proteins; the difference between fructose and legumes. Don't waste your money on junk food and empty calories. (See the glossary entry on Cooking.)

Overdraft Protection
Before banking went online, an overdraft occurred when someone wrote out a check for more money than they had in their bank account. If an overdraft occurred, the bank returned the check to the depositor and charged a fee. The person who created the overdraft was said to have "bounced" a check. A person who bounced a check was liable to pay the original amount plus the bank fee to the depositor and an additional fee. Some banks offered their customers "overdraft protection." Banks would cash the check, possibly charge a fee, and allow the customer to deposit additional funds to cover the overdraft.

With electronic banking, it is still possible to write paper checks and create overdrafts. It is also possible to schedule an electronic payment and lack sufficient funds to cover the payment. So banks continue to offer forms of overdraft protection. Banks may continue to charge fees. This is an area where you have to pay attention to the details. It's also an example of why it's so important to follow Rule No. 1 and save money. The best kind of overdraft protection allows the bank to withdraw funds from your savings account if there are insufficient funds in your checking account. You receive notification, but at least at some banks and credit unions, there are no additional fees. These are the kinds of details you need to study when deciding where to keep money.

Passbook Savings Account
An old, old form of savings account. Your records of savings deposits and withdrawals are recorded in a little booklet you can keep in a shirt pocket. Typically, you have to go into the financial institution to transact business. For people who are just getting back on their feet financially, this may be the only kind of savings account that is available. It's old-fashioned, but it works. You're better off working with a credit union or bank that offers a full set of online banking services. If you don't have access to that, a passbook savings

The Rules

account can get you started in following Rule No. 1.

Pocket Money

When you consider spending plans, it is important to include some *pocket money* that you may spend on "whatever." Maybe it's a lunch out or a beer after work or a graphic novel or ice cream with the kids. You can't plan for every penny you are going to spend. You need to account for that, but do it within limits. Have realistic expectations. Give yourself some latitude within them.

Portfolio

Stockbrokers and investment advisors refer to an individual's collection of stocks, bonds, funds, and similar investments as the individual's portfolio. Professional advisors recommend a mix of investments. They talk about "balancing your portfolio."

Power of Attorney

A *power of attorney* (POA) is a legal document that gives someone else the ability to make legal decisions for you in case you are incapacitated by illness or injury. It, along with a living will, is something you need—just in case—to make life easier for the people closest to you. All documents like this must be properly signed (with witnesses) and notarized to be legally binding.

Practice Routines

If you want to learn to play a sport, develop skill in a game like chess, or learn to play a musical instrument, there are two important things you must do. First you have to learn the rules, the movements, and all the basic elements of the skill you want to develop. Then you have to practice. And practice some more. And some more. Do the same thing the same way until it becomes automatic. The same fundamentals apply to taking proper care of your money. Remember Rule No. 5. Learn to do the right thing the right way. Then do it again. And again. And again. Practice.

Premium

The *premium* is the insurance-industry term for the price you pay for the protection you are purchasing. With vehicle insurance and term life insurance, for example, the premium is a simple price tag. With some other forms of insurance, such as whole life insurance, it may be thought of as a kind of investment. For your spending plans, it's the money you have to spend to keep your insurance protection in place.

Prepaid (Secured) Credit or Debit Cards

You put up the cash and you get a credit card with a credit limit up to the amount paid into the account. Technically, these are all debit cards. The "charge" is deducted from your account balance at the time of each transaction. You can't spend beyond your credit limit and you don't have to worry about paying off your balance every billing cycle. Instead, you must add money to the account to fund future purchases.

Some of these cards allow you to start borrowing more money than you have in your account after a waiting period. Presto, the issuers magically turned it into a credit card. Now you can borrow money and they then charge you interest. If you are following Rule No. 4, you must be very careful. These kinds of accounts may not require a credit check, so a prepaid credit card can be a useful tool to use when you are establishing or reestablishing your credit. Prepaid debit cards frequently charge fees. Shop carefully for a card that does not have any additional hidden fees or other gotchas.

Prime Rate

The interest rate that commercial banks charge their best customers. The Federal Reserve (Fed) sets the federal funds' overnight rate, which is used as the basis for the prime rate. The prime rate is used as the starting point for loan and credit card interest rates. A mortgage loan interest rate might be set as prime rate plus 3 percent, for example. When the prime rate changes, the mortgage rate changes.

Principal
A number that appears on a mortgage or loan statement, the principal represents the amount of your payment that goes toward repaying the amount you borrowed and reducing the amount of money you owe. If you make a full mortgage payment, you pay principal and interest (and possibly escrow and fees). If you want to pay the mortgage off faster and pay less interest, you could include some additional money to be applied to the principal. The balance on the loan is reduced. Your next interest payment will be smaller, so a greater percentage of your next payment will go toward principal. That's why paying principal is like putting money in your own pocket.

Probate
The legal proceedings that are involved in assuring that a deceased person's will is properly prepared and legally binding. When probate is completed, the executor of the deceased person's estate is able to distribute the proceeds to the deceased person's beneficiaries. If a person does not have a will (dies intestate) an executor is appointed by the court, the estate goes through probate, and state laws apply in determining the distribution of the estate.

Recurring Costs
It's the drip, drip, drip of spending. Certainly there is a (usually) monthly bill for housing (rent or mortgage). Maybe you have to pay for electricity or water or Internet service every month. The challenge, if you want to keep more of your money, is to minimize these kinds of payments. Telephone services (mobile and landline) via an Internet connection are available for much less than the standard monthly fees big utilities provide; even less if you pay annually. Cable television can be fairly said to be a rip-off, as millions of "cord cutters" are deciding every year. When you follow Rule No. 4 and get rid of that car payment, it makes a huge difference. But look for little recurring costs, too. Every time you identify something you pay for every day, week, month, or year, think hard about it. Is there a less costly alternative? Is it really necessary at all?

Risk Averse
How comfortable are you with the prospect of losing money? If a drop in the stock market that reduces the value of your investments deeply disturbs you, you can be said to be risk averse. If the possibility of "losing" a lot of money, even if it is only theoretical, doesn't concern you, then you may be said to be risk tolerant. You can easily find many risk assessment or risk tolerance quizzes online. Visit a few. Don't buy anything—these tests are all promotional come-ons—but do think about the results and develop a better understanding of how you really feel about possible financial gains or losses.

Risk Management
The insurance industry says the general purpose of insurance is to "manage" your risk. With automobile insurance, you may have no choice about whether to buy a policy or not, but you still have to make decisions about deductibles and the amount of coverage, which affect the price. Health insurance? Life insurance? You have to think about them to protect yourself and those close to you. When you live by *The Rules* and start saving money, you have more things you want to protect. That's risk management.

Risk/Reward
People talk about risk and reward, sometimes saying you have to take bigger risks to get bigger rewards. See Rule No. 7—investing and insurance are like gambling. You can place a big bet and maybe get lucky. And maybe not.

Here's one thing you can count on: Slow and steady moves you forward. Savings accounts and certificates of deposit are completely safe. Investments in big, diversified funds like an S&P 500 index fund are unlikely to crash and will probably grow. You do not need to make big, risky bets to get ahead.

Routing Number

Every credit union or bank has a unique number that is used to identify it within the banking system. When you set up direct deposit, link a high-interest savings account to your bank account, or establish financial monitoring on a site like mint.com, you need to know your institution's routing number (in addition to your own account number). Typically you can find it on the organization's web pages or with an Internet search.

Savings Account

This account is the most boring, least profitable place to put your money. It is so boring that you never have to worry about losing it, it is always available if you need access to it, and while it won't earn a lot of interest, it also will never lose money. Experts say that when inflation goes up, the value of your savings goes down. Theoretically, that is true, but only if you are spending the money. If you are saving it, you might not be able to buy as much of something in a year, but you still have your money and you are in a better position to shop, find bargains, and make good decisions about what you want to do with your money. Never underestimate the value of a good old, boring, savings account.

Savings Buckets

Bucket is an accounting term used to indicate separate categories or accounts where you can assign income or debt. With online banking, you probably have a few buckets that appear automatically. Your checking account might be automatically linked to a savings account, for example. Possibly there is a money market account. You can use these additional accounts for your own purposes: "emergency savings," for one, "travel/vacation" for another, or "car maintenance/replacement." Then you can apply Rule No. 1: Pay Yourself First. Make these buckets into places where you put your savings. It is easy to know exactly where you stand and how much you can spend when you put your money into buckets like that.

Simplifying Your Life (The Right Way)

Artists and designers frequently create works of art that are extremely simple. Ordinary people can live lives with a similar aesthetic. If you can focus more on the most important things in your life (Rule No. 9) and worry less about having stuff, it can be a major step toward reducing stress and bringing your life into a comfortable balance.

True simplicity in life is getting rid of debts and not adding any new ones.

SMART Goals

SMART is an acronym with each letter standing for a condition to apply to a plan. S is for *specific* (can what you want to do be stated clearly?). M is for *measurable* (how will you know if you accomplished your goal?). A is for *achievable* (can it really be done?). R is for *relevant* (does it matter?). T is for *time-bound* (when will it happen?). Some people make them SMARTER goals by adding E for *evaluated* and R for *reviewed*.

SMART goals are a good idea. They are the difference between "I need to save some money to take care of things that might come up" and "I plan to save my lunch money every day for the next six months so that I have at least $500 in my emergency savings fund—check back with me in three months to see how I'm doing, and in six months we can go out for a pizza to celebrate." Which goal is more likely to get accomplished?

When you set goals for yourself, make them Specific, Measurable, Achievable, and Relevant, and give yourself a Time when you plan to get the job done.

Spending Plan

When you think about your money and where it goes, use the term "spending plan" instead of "budget." The B-word is negative. It suggests that you are going to write everything down and track it and account for every penny. And in the end, you wouldn't do most of that stuff, and you'd probably feel bad about it.

A spending plan focuses on the most important part of the budgeting process—deciding where your money is going to go. It may seem like the same thing as creating a budget, but it has a more active, positive focus.

Spirituality

Some people may feel that contributing to a religious group is their highest priority. This book argues that Rule No. 1 still applies. No matter how strongly you feel about your religion, you need to attend to your own financial health to be able to continue to support your family, your religion, or anything else.

It is also worth considering that some spiritual practices—attending services, meditation or even something like yoga—can be a great help when you're under stress. If you are in debt and have to make financial sacrifices, strengthening your spiritual base may prove to be a great help to you. Remember Rule No. 9 and Rule No. 10.

State Laws Concerning Estates

(See Probate.)

Student Loans

Loans for education can be dangerous, for students and for parents. Read Appendix B. Be careful. Remember Rule No. 4.

Subprime Loan

Subprime loans are loans made to people who do not qualify for the best loan interest rates. Subprime loan interest rates are actually much higher than the prime interest rate. The term "subprime" refers to the person borrowing the money, not to the loan rate. Subprime borrowers may be people rejected by traditional lenders because of low credit scores, or for other reasons that suggest the borrower may not be able to pay back the loan.

The two biggest markets for subprime loans are mortgages and car loans. Finance companies target people with low credit ratings and charge very high interest rates. While it is true there is greater risk for the lender, this has proved to be very profitable for the finance industry. Even if a customer defaults, the lenders have the real estate or the vehicle as collateral. The borrowers, failing to follow Rule No. 4, are the ones who pay the biggest price for these kinds of loans.

Sucker Bet

If it seems too good to be true, it usually is. If you think you deserve to keep more of your money, do not be foolish and give it away or lose it on a sucker bet. Be especially careful when dealing with friends or members of your family. If you give someone money, think of it as a gift, not a loan. Be prepared to never get it back.

Taxability of Insurance Proceeds

Most insurance claim payments are not taxable. If you come into a large amount of money through an insurance claim, find and pay an expert to advise you on the tax implications and other matters.

Tax-Advantaged

The idea behind *tax-advantaged* benefits is that you don't pay taxes right away, when your tax rate is theoretically higher, and you end up paying the taxes later (like when you retire) and your taxes are theoretically lower. Some tax-advantaged benefits let you pay for services like day care with "before tax" dollars—you never have to pay any federal tax at all on that income. Tax-advantaged plans work best for highly paid employees. They matter less to people earning an average income, but they may still be helpful. So, if you work at a company that offers tax-advantaged benefits like 401(k) plans or flexible spending accounts (FSAs), be sure to learn about how they might benefit you.

Term Life Insurance

The purpose of insurance is to protect family members from lost income. The "term" in *term life insurance* refers to the length of time the person buying the coverage can leave a guaranteed amount to their family if they die. If, at age 25, someone purchases a 15-year term life insurance policy, the person can keep renewing the policy by paying the premium until reaching 40 years of age, regardless of changes in the insured person's health. Typically, a medical examination is required before you will be issued a term life insurance policy. Term insurance protection ends if a premium payment isn't made on time, even during the initially agreed term. A person can open a new policy even if another policy is in place, but that probably requires another health examination. Term life insurance is relatively inexpensive for young healthy people. It gets more expensive as people get older, if they have health conditions, or if they smoke.

Terms and Conditions

Read the fine print. Any time you sign an agreement, especially one that has been prepared by someone else for you, you need to study. If it is important, invest in the services of an attorney to review it. If you sign up for a student loan, read all the terms and conditions. If something happens later that you might have avoided, you'll have only yourself to blame.

Tightwad

Not a bad thing to be. See the glossary entry for *cheapskate*.

Tracking Your Success

See the glossary entry for *Keeping Score*.

Transaction Fees

Any time money changes hands in the financial service industry, it is likely that someone is paying some sort of *transaction fee*. For example, when a customer uses a credit card to make a purchase at a store, the merchant typically pays a fixed charge for the transaction plus a percentage of the amount charged. The processing fee can include interchange fees, assessment fees, and payment fees that can add up to about 3.5 percent of the total amount of the charge. Debit cards have lower processing fees—sometimes less than 1 percent.

All of this is invisible to customers, but it does matter to merchants and helps explain some policies. As responsible card users, it is helpful to understand that in the world of financial services, everyone involved is looking for a piece of the action. See the glossary entry for *vigorish*.

Understanding Marketing

Remember this—imprint it on your brain in big, glowing letters—*everyone* wants you to give them your money. If you turn on a television, listen to the radio, look at a computer, walk down a busy street, open your mail, read a magazine, go to an entertainment event, or even spend time sitting in a waiting room, you will be bombarded with images and messages designed to make you want stuff and give other people your money. And if you do get the stuff they are selling, you'll get more messages and more encouragement to get more stuff. It never ends.

Fight back. Armor yourself against all the messages—the advertising and marketing and influencing. They all want your money. Don't give it to them.

Underwater

When the balance of a loan is greater than the value of the asset you purchased with the loan you are underwater. This happens most frequently when someone makes a poor decision and borrows a lot of money to buy an asset (like a vehicle) that loses value very quickly. It may also occur in real estate when there is a "price correction" in the housing market. Someone takes out a mortgage for a property valued at $300,000. Prices drop in the housing market, as they did in 2008. The property is suddenly worth only $200,000. The mortgage holder owes far more than that and is suddenly underwater.

Variable Costs and Expenses

Spending plans need to include the resources to deal with variable expenses—costs that may go up or down depending on the time of the year, your work opportunities, big changes in the overall economy (such as sudden increases in gas prices), or other factors that are out of your control. Your emergency savings fund is one buffer against these sorts of expenses. You also need to be realistic about expenses. Plan in advance—think about the year ahead and build in a cushion. A little pain now can save a lot of pain later.

Vesting

An investment term related to pensions, stock options and, more frequently today, 401(k) and similar retirement plans. With a 401(k) plan, for example, an employer may make a matching contribution to your fund. If you contribute 2 percent of your income, the employer contributes a matching 2 percent. At the end of a year, you may look at your statement and see a nice total sum in your account. But if your 401(k) plan has a vesting requirement, you may not be able to keep all that money if you leave that job. A vesting requirement might entitle you to 20 percent of the company contribution after one year, 40 percent after two years, and so on. After five years of employment, you might be "fully vested" and be able to keep all the money in your fund if you leave the employer. Check with the human resources representative to learn how long you must work the job to receive the full employer match.

You always get to keep the money you contribute to the fund. Only the employer's contributions are affected by vesting.

Vigorish (Vig)

The street tough's term for interest. It is associated with loan sharks and rough business. It seems appropriate, however, for a lot of financial operations today—payday loans, check cashers, and rent-to-own stores, certainly. But you can add any financial services company into the mix when you look at the money they make on penalties, overdraft fees, late charges, and high interest.

Whole Life Insurance

A form of life insurance that has a relatively high premium and low benefit, but that also serves as a kind of investment. You can keep it in force throughout your life and the premium stays the same. The insurance grows in cash value, and you can borrow money against it. It's complicated (compared to a term life policy). It requires the kind of study that you might put into any other major investment decision. (*See also* Term Life Insurance.)

Will

A legal document that provides guidance to the people closest to you concerning your last wishes. This may include the distribution of any assets (money or property), decisions about the disposition of your remains (burial? cremation?), and your feelings about how you would like to be remembered. Also, see the glossary entries for Living Will and Power of Attorney. You need to prepare these legal documents, too. There are free online tools that you can use to create these documents and make life easier for everyone around you. All documents like this must be properly signed (with witnesses) and notarized to be legally binding.

Windfall

A financial windfall is the arrival of a lot of money—hundreds, thousands, maybe even more. There are some windfalls you can anticipate, like income tax refunds. Others are unexpected, like receiving an inheritance or an unanticipated year-end bonus. With any of these kinds of events, you suddenly have access to a lot of money. You need to make up your mind in advance that you're NOT going to let people take all that money away from you. Plan ahead—if you get a windfall, what percentage will go into savings? Which buckets will it go into? Then consider any debts you want to get rid of.

Then—after you have taken care of business—you can think about treating yourself or your family to something. Celebrate. Give yourself a small reward at the same time that you are following Rule No. 1.

The Rules

Part V
Parting Shots

Support Plans, Encouragement Extra Credit, Resources, and More

A Few More Words of Wisdom

*Too many people spend money they earned
to buy things they don't want
to impress people that they don't like.*
Will Rogers

*Wealth consists not in having great possessions,
but in having few wants.*
Epictetus

*The real measure of your wealth is how much
you'd be worth if you lost all your money.*
Anonymous

Wealth is the ability to fully experience life.
Henry David Thoreau

*It's not the load that breaks you down.
It's the way you carry it.*
Lena Horne

*Winning is great, sure, but if you are really
going to do something in life, the secret is
learning how to lose. Nobody goes undefeated
all the time. If you can pick up after a crushing
defeat and go on to win again, you are going to
be a champion someday.*
Wilma Rudolph

*The battles that count aren't the ones for
gold medals. The struggles within
yourself—the invisible, inevitable battles
inside all of us—that's where it's at.*
Jesse Owens

Clear eyes. Full heart. Can't lose.
Peter Berg

A Letter from an Old Man

Dear Reader,

Congrats. You made it this far. I'm impressed.

Of course, we all still have a long way to go.

I'm an old man. I've seen a lot of changes over the years. I remember regular five and a quarter percent interest on savings accounts, paper saving bonds, and real, genuine pension plans. I've watched government and big business wage an assault on unions, I've seen the deterioration of all kinds of workers' rights, and I am well aware of the unchecked growth of financial inequality in our country.

It's not a pretty sight. And yet, that's what you have to cope with.

When I first got involved with this project—everything that has led up to this book and *The Rules*—I saw a very well-intentioned effort to promote something people called "financial literacy."

I hate that term—"financial literacy." The people I know, even five-year-olds, are not financially "illiterate." They understand all the basics of buying and selling stuff. That part is easy.

No—we are all financially literate.

The problems arise when scientifically designed, tremendously effective marketing is combined with finely tuned, highly profitable financial services. Economists look at the United States and say that we live in a "consumer economy." Big business and big finance like that idea. If we go out and "consume" more, they make more money. The result is pressure on us to buy more stuff and to go into debt to do it.

If you're thinking about the future and topics like investing and insurance, the financial services industry employs all the tools of modern marketing. Simple options barely exist. Instead, we are left to try to find our way through massive amounts of information. Either that or listen to what the company representatives say, make the best choices we can, and hope for the best.

The Rich get Richer.

Big business and big finance want to make it easy for us to consume. And they want to be sure that when we consume, they get paid. So they design all the consumer-related rules and regulations to make it easy to go into debt, hard to pay off debt, and extremely difficult to get rid of debt through bankruptcy.

As I said in the beginning of this book, the system is rigged.

In the early 2000s, when I was teaching the Money Class at a halfway house, I met people who faced enormous personal financial challenges. They were not financially "illiterate." They were caught up in an unfair system and being set up to fail.

So I got involved in trying find a way to help. To sort through the Boring Stuff and provide people with tools that they could use to get out from under their burdens and live free and clear. That's how *The Rules* evolved.

But there's more.

One of the first things I learned when well-intentioned people came in and did a presentation was that one class wasn't enough. It takes time to sort through all the Boring Stuff and figure out what is really important. It takes time to learn *The Rules* and really understand what they mean. It takes time to learn how to use them—to apply them to you own situation.

So I made a promise to myself. No one-shot deals.

If I was going to get involved with this, it had to be for the long run. This kind of work takes time. And it takes lots of practice. (Rule No. 5). You've got to be willing to stay committed for the long haul. That's what I told myself.

So I kept at it. I even wrote a couple of books.

But . . . reading a book—that's a kind of one-shot deal. Even if you study it in a class. Break everything down. Get some practice. Even if you have the book to refer back to from time to time. When I thought about it, I had to say "that's not enough."

So here's what we are doing. We are taking advantage of the Internet (a nod to Rule No. 6) and providing readers with resources you can use at any time going forward. The only requirement for taking full advantage of them is to have an email address.

First, there is a website. Visit www.moneyandwealth.org and you'll find information and links to important things such as a full color, frame-able copy of *The Rules* and the FTC-recommended form for requesting a free copy of your credit report.

Second, you will find an invitation to subscribe to *The Money Class*—a newsletter/discussion list. Subscribing to it does two things for you. You will receive regular issues of the newsletter and occasional special stories and announcements. Plus—the discussion list allows you to post comments and ask questions. You'll be able to communicate with the people involved in creating *The Rules* and share your thoughts with a growing online community. There will be more about this in the following section covering *Resources*.

Again, congratulations on reaching this point in the book. Yes, you had to wade through some Boring Stuff along the way, I know. I'm sorry. But with money and wealth it always happens—there are details you have to pay attention to and some of that stuff is boring. That's just how it is.

Sincerely,

Ridge

How to Get the Most Out of This Book

Two ideas for how people can learn about money management have been present from the beginning of the work that produced *The Rules* and this book.

First: People have a lot of experience working with money already and they are not going to do anything differently just because someone tells them something. Experts, teachers, group leaders, and people like that can *say* students should do something, but the effect of that will be very limited.

From the very beginning, our idea was to encourage students to *talk with each other* about *The Rules* and the rest of the ideas presented in the book. We wanted students to discuss the material, exchange views, and, in the end, *to convince each other* that the No B.S. Rules approach has merit—that it's the right way to go and it will be worth the effort and even the sacrifices it will take.

If you are in a class, we hope you have had this kind of "discuss things and learn together" experience.

If you're reading this book by yourself, we recommend that you talk about the ideas in it with others. If you have a partner, it could be a great icebreaker for some really important conversations about money. Or you could talk about it with a close friend, or a book group, or . . . ? The idea is to go beyond the words on the page, say *The Rules* out loud, maybe challenge them, unpack some of your preconceptions, and even make some public commitments to *take action,* as the book suggests.

Challenge Yourself with Scenarios

Our lesson plans for classes using *The Rules* always include scenarios. The idea is to encourage students to consider a situation that has been suggested and decide which rules should be applied. The students can redefine the situation, elaborate on it, and offer a variety of suggestions for how to apply *The Rules*. The idea behind the scenarios is to encourage this kind of thinking.

The scenarios are a reflection of real life. Every person's situation is different. We want the students to know *The Rules* very well (ideally, be able to identify them by number immediately) and think about how they might apply them. Our reason for doing this? We hope, in the future, this way of analyzing situations will carry through into the students' lives as they face real-world problems.

If you are up to the challenge, we are including some scenarios here for your consideration. Give yourself extra credit for tackling them. Give yourself double extra credit if you take on the challenge in the company of a partner or friend(s) and discuss your different approaches.

Scenarios

How Would You Apply *The Rules*?

Consider the following financial and finance-related situations. Think about and discuss how someone who follows *The Rules* would approach them. Which rules apply? What would you do?

1) You receive a credit card offer. It has a fairly low interest rate and offers "cash advances" at a slightly higher rate. And you can get a $200 bonus if you use it 10 times a month for the next three months.

2) You live in a cold climate. Winter is coming. You don't have a winter jacket, hat, and gloves.

3) The Lotto jackpot is more than $10 million.

4) Your doctor prescribed a statin drug, Lipitor, to help control your cholesterol level. It's time to refill the prescription, but it is really expensive.

5) The car you're driving is very shabby. It runs okay, but it needs new brakes and new tires, and probably a battery soon. You see an offer to lease a new car for only $99 down and $200 a month.

6) It is your wife's birthday and you'd like to take her out to dinner and give her a very nice present. But that would be expensive.

7) You have an emergency fund equal to three months' worth of your expenses. Your old television stops working. What do you do?

8) You don't have a great relationship with your child, but the weather is nice and you're not working today.

9) A favorite aunt passed away and left $2,500 to you in her will. You just received the check.

10) You want to open a checking account. The bank you talk to has a $5 monthly fee if your account has less than $500.

11) You promised your family to take a trip to the beach on your day off. But now your boss tells you that you can get overtime pay if you come to work.

12) You're eligible for a 401(k) plan that matches your contributions for up to 4 percent of your pay.

13) You really like to watch (name of some sport here) but it's only available on ESPN. And to get ESPN, it seems like you have to buy a cable service that costs $79 a month, plus taxes and other fees. What do you do?

14) You're thinking about taking a computer programming course that promises a high-paying job. But it is pretty expensive. People at the school say you will qualify for financial aid—no problems. You do have a good Internet connection at home.

15) When you get your paycheck, you have to take it to a check-cashing business that charges you 1.99 percent.

16) Things are going well. Your emergency fund is set. You have a family. You have one or two young children. You just got a promotion, and a nice raise came along with it.

17) You haven't met your goal for your emergency savings, but you see a really nice, stylish jacket that would look great on you.

18) You are filling out forms for a driver's license and you find a question about becoming an organ donor.

19) You've got a savings account and you are trying to get your emergency savings fund together, but you never seem to make any progress.

20) You see an ad for a "technical institute" that offers a class in cybersecurity. The ad says you can earn at least $50,000 a year after taking the class.

Get Involved

You've read this far—you already know that this book has kind of an attitude problem.

We're not looking at the world as it is and saying everything is great; we say the system is rigged.

Not only is it rigged, but for some people, the "terms and conditions" of life seem to be designed, on purpose, to make them fail.

Our goal, in this book, has been to encourage everyone—even people facing the longest odds—that they can succeed. If you work hard and follow *The Rules*, you can get ahead with your personal finances. You can reduce your stress about money. You can spend less time thinking about financial Boring Stuff and more time focusing on things that really matter.

And in our view, one of the things that really matters is doing work to fix this kind of broken, messed-up, rigged economic system we have in the United States.

You, all alone, are not likely to have much of an impact. But, if you find people and organizations that are working on the problems, you can have an impact.

If you can, register to vote. Educate yourself. Find out what the people who are running for office think and plan to do for people like you. Work for candidates you believe in. Every vote counts.

Join organizations working for the kinds of policies and goals that you believe in. Individuals, unless they are very wealthy, can't make a big difference in politics and policy making. Organizations—with ten or fifty or a hundred or a thousand people—they can get attention. They can become a movement, and they can make a big difference.

If you have the opportunity, support and join a union. If you read up on the history of unions in the United States, you will find that in the post-World War II era (late 1940s and the 1950s) when union participation was at its highest level, real income for all workers rose, and income inequality went down. Unions helped raise wages and benefits for their members, and things got a little better for everyone else in the country.

Be a volunteer. Work in food drives and shelters; get involved in animal rescue organizations; coach a youth sports team; work to help save the environment and fight climate change; and look for opportunities to meet new people, make friends, and make the world a little bit better and a more welcoming place.

Rule No. 8—things never stay the same. This old world is always getting better or getting worse. Follow the rule. Make the world better for yourself, your loved ones, for all of us.

Stone Soup—A Recipe

Throughout this book you've seen references to things that may seem completely unrelated to money and personal financial management. If you skipped over the entries in the Glossary for Cooking or Mindfulness and Meditation, go back and check them out. (It's okay that you skipped them—they *are* part of the Boring Stuff.)

Here is a suggested exercise that seems, on the surface, to be unrelated to personal finance and *The Rules*. But read on. There's an explanation.

Stone Soup

Ingredients:

One stone

Some olive oil or whatever cooking oil you use.

Salt (Diamond Crystal Kosher salt is preferred).

Pepper (We find that Tabasco sauce, added a few drops at a time, is a good substitute).

Soy sauce or Worcestershire sauce or a couple of anchovies (Something with an umami hit, if you have it).

Whatever ingredients your guests bring with them.

Advance Preparation (several days):

1. Get your family—spouse, significant other, kids, roommates, hangers on—on board. Figure out a good time and place. Explain that we are going to make stone soup. When they come, they have to bring something to add to the pot.

2. Suggest some sample ingredients. A potato, some carrots, green beans, a can of diced tomatoes, a zucchini, a yam or sweet potato, a bit of squash, an ear of corn, some frozen peas . . . whatever. I suggest you keep it vegetarian, so no meats please. But a bit or rice would be nice, or some pearled barley, farro, or bulgur, or teeny tiny pasta stars. An old cheese rind would be a great addition if you don't mind the soup being non-vegan.

3. Then invite some more friends and family. And maybe that new neighbor you haven't met from across the street or that really shy-seeming person who lives down the hall.

More Advance Preparation:

1. Find a nice stone. A stone that weighs about eight to ten ounces will work well but it can be larger or smaller. A river stone that has been

worn smooth by years spent in running water is preferred. It will give the soup a smoother consistency and add more "juice" to the pot.

2. Place the stone in a small pot and cover with water. Salt the water—about a teaspoon of salt will do. Heat the water to a boil and simmer for at least 15 minutes. This process helps concentrate the juices in the stone.

3. When the stone is done (it will still be firm to the touch, but salt and hot water will have worked their magic) remove it from the water, let it cool briefly and store it in a food-safe container in the refrigerator until it is time to make the soup. Discard the cooking water.

4. Be sure you have a big pot. You may have to borrow one. A BIG pot. Big enough for soup for everyone.

Making the Soup

1. Put your big pot on the stove. Add a couple of quarts of water and start heating it.

2. With great ceremony (gather everyone around) place your carefully prepared stone in the pot.

3. Dice up your onions. Go for a very fine dice, but chunks and big bits are okay, too. Put 'em in a frying pan and cook them until they are translucent. A little browning is okay, too; just don't let them burn. (Chances are pretty good that someone will bring an onion or two, but I suggest you have two or three big yellow onions on hand just in case. [This is NOT cheating. It's our recipe and we make up the rules.])

4. As people arrive with ingredients, prep them to go into the soup. Peel, slice, and dice them up. Put them in little bowls or heap them on plates.

5. Add ingredients based on the amount of time they need to cook. Green beans and rice take a long time. If you like a bit of crunch in your celery, add it right at the end (someone will bring celery, for sure). Consult with your sous-chefs. Have fun.

6. Serve with some sides: crusty bread, hummus, salsa and chips—whatever is at hand. Plus beverages of choice.

After You Eat

You'll probably have leftovers. Share them with guests.

As for the stone, there are two schools of thought.

Some people think that once a stone is used as a soup stone, it loses some of its flavor, becomes a little tender and shriveled, and will never make really great soup again. Other people think that a good soup stone is revitalized in the cooking process, filled with extra juices and flavor from the ingredients, and can be preserved and used for generations.

I'm in the "lasts forever" camp myself. Do some taste testing and learn from experience to decide what you think.

What Does Stone Soup Have to Do with Personal Financial Management?

First, you are following *The Rules*; especially Rules No. 2, No. 9, and No. 10. You are spending less for a big dinner by sharing the costs with friends. You are enjoying some of your non-monetary wealth: the company of family and friends (and possibly making new friends). You are gathering your team. As the dinner progresses, you'll probably talk about the stone soup, where you got the idea, *The Rules,* and things you are working on.

And an Even Bigger Picture

It is human nature to try to separate our problems and deal with things one at a time. We want to fix things, to solve a problem, and to get on with the rest of our lives. It would be nice, but in reality everything we do is connected somehow to everything else. And money is a big factor in all that.

Money helps shape our choices in food, shelter, and clothing. Money impacts our healthcare decisions. Money causes stress and anxiety for a lot of people.

In *The No B.S. Rules* we have tried to acknowledge that reality. *The Rules* certainly focus on money and what we do with it. At the same time, they encourage us to pay attention to other aspects of our lives, our life priorities, and (Rule No. 9) what REALLY matters.

You can't separate the "money thing" from everything else in life. What you can do is put it in perspective.

Think about it.

Somewhere Everything is Connected to Everything Has to Go

And the next really nice day you have, go outside and look around. (Cliché alert!) Smell the dang roses. And keep your eyes open for a nice smooth stone that might be just right for a big pot of stone soup.

The Rules

Resources

Other Books

You want to read another book?

There are thousands of books about personal financial planning and investing available. They offer information and advice in hundreds of different flavors and formats. The key is to find books that speak to you and your needs.

Start your search at your local public library. Find the right section and start browsing. Maybe one of the "For Dummies" books is right for you? Take out a few books. See if you can find an author who engages your interest and encourages you to go on before you shell out any of your hard-earned money to buy one.

Michelle Singletary works at *The Washington Post* and has written several smart, thoughtful, and practical books. Suze Orman, a popular financial advisor on radio and television, also has a website with useful resources. Dave Ramsey's books seem good to me, but he includes a strong religious component in his advice, and his website seems too interested in selling stuff.

For one book on investing, check out *A Random Walk Down Wall Street* by Burton G. Malkiel. Straight talk advocating index funds, diversification, and patience.

Plus, here is one specific specific book recommendation.

The Richest Man in New Babylon
Ridge Kennedy, Hedgehog House Books

If you want to go to the source for *The Rules*, read *The Richest Man in New Babylon*. It presents *The Rules* in the context of a story of a young man facing tremendous challenges. He meets people. He learns *The Rules*. It makes a difference for him. You will have to buy this book online. Look for the *Classroom Edition*. It should be less expensive and includes some new information in the *Afterwords* section.

Websites

Information You Can Trust

The Money and Wealth Website: Home Base for *The Rules*
moneyandwealth.org

Visit the site and sign up for *The Money Class* newsletter. It will provide useful information and give you the opportunity to comment, ask questions, and engage with other people who are traveling with you on a similar journey.

Internal Revenue Service (IRS): www.irs.gov

Information about free tax filing (IRS Free File), volunteer tax assistance (VITA), and help with any other tax-related questions. Also a resource for information about 401(k) and similar plans, IRAs, Roth IRAs, the Earned Income Tax Credit (EITC), and more.

Federal Trade Commission (FTC): www.ftc.gov and www.consumer.ftc.gov

Information about credit reports, credit freezes, and all things credit related. Also home of the "do-not-call" list, information about preventing identity theft, and other helpful personal finance information.

Consumer Financial Protection Bureau (CFPB): www.cfpb.gov

Another source for information about consumer credit and consumer protection. The CFPB offers consumer-friendly educational material for personal financial management (leaders' guides and handouts for students). Much of the CFPB educational material is available in Spanish.

Department of the Treasury: treasury.gov and treasurydirect.gov

The Treasury Department generally operates in the stratosphere of the financial world, where decisions impact the entire U.S. economy. But there is one service it offers with a direct benefit to consumers—especially savers. Individuals can purchase government savings bonds at www.treasurydirect.gov. You will find information about how to buy Series I, Series EE, and other government-backed securities.

This can be fairly complicated. But if you simply want to be a well-informed saver and investor, treasurydirect.com is a site worth exploring.

Other Financial Sites?

Thousands of Internet websites provide free financial advice. Can you trust them? Remember the wise person's warning: You get what you pay for.

Find reviews of sites, visit and browse them, and generally see "what's out there." Remember: Most of these sites are earning income in some way. They have advertisements and sponsored links. They sell stuff—books and "special access" to website features and classes. Beware!

When you are looking for information about a specific topic, seek out multiple sources for the same information. If all of them agree, then you can be a little more confident in the accuracy of the information they provide. If you find useful information, use it. But be very, very careful. Like everyone else out there, these people want to take your money. Don't let them.

E-conomy: Access to Online Financial Services

This is an opinion. Big screens help.

Online service providers are emphasizing their availability on smartphones. The idea is appealing, and there are times when having access to your bank account via your phone is helpful. But consider the risks. If you lose your phone, you lose access to your accounts and, depending on your phone's security, you may open yourself to fraud.

More important in our opinion, however, is giving yourself a full view of your finances. You can't do that on a phone screen.

The larger screen of a tablet is better than a smartphone screen. But really, for the best view of your data and ease of working with it, the additional screen size and physical keyboard of a computer will serve you best. A full-sized computer screen gives you a bigger picture. It allows you to see much more information at one time. Setting up automation routines is much easier using a keyboard and mouse rather than a touch screen. It can also be helpful to have a printer.

All things considered, a big screen gives you more perspective on everything you are doing.

Shared computers: If you need to use a shared computer or public access computer like one in a library, pay extra attention to security. Do NOT allow internet browsers to save your login names and passwords.

E-conomy: Online Banking

You have many good options. Any decent-sized financial institution probably has a solid online platform that offers good account access, online bill payment, remote deposit, and a suite of other features. To keep your costs as low as possible, we recommend considering credit unions as well as banks.

The Navy Federal Credit Union is the nation's largest credit union, and it is open to anyone who has served in the military (or worked for some other government agencies) and their families.

Residents of New Jersey and its environs can look into the Affinity Federal Credit Union. (It is the author's "home team.")

Another institution: Consumer's Credit Union (myconsumers.org) offers membership to all members of the Consumers Cooperative Association. Anyone can join the association for a $5 fee. Consumers Credit Union is based in Chicago, where it has numerous branches. Additionally, it has thousands of fee-free ATMs and shared service locations nationwide.

Do your research. Select a financial service provider with low costs and great online services.

E-conomy: Online Financial Management/Tracking

It is difficult to do this manually. You would need to check balances for all your accounts, write down the information, and do the math. An online financial application automates the entire process (Rule No. 6).

Which program to choose? We have had good success and are happy with mint.com. However, there are many alternatives available. Do research, and look for the program or app that is right for you. Our criteria are as follows:

- Free (or comes with enough benefits that you think it is a good value).
- Can be linked to bank, credit card, and other accounts (especially mortgage).
- Allows you to manually add assets or liabilities that are not accessible online.
- Updates online accounts automatically.
- Does not include too many ads or marketing messages.

Some of these kinds of programs allow you to categorize and "tag" payments in ways that allow you to see very clearly how much you are spending on things like transportation, clothing, dining out and so forth. That can be useful, if you want to do it.

The Rules focus on the totals. How are you going to keep score? How much have you saved? What is your "equity"? After you link all your accounts, a service like mint.com will provide you with a single number for your "net worth."

E-conomy: Online Resources for Creating Wills, Living Wills, and Estate Documents

One site, freewill.com, provides completely free estate planning tools including wills, trusts, beneficiary designations, advance healthcare directives (living wills), charitable distributions, stock donations, and power of attorney documents. The site is supported by charities that pay a fee to freewill.com to have their names included for possible donations. However, no donations are required to use the site's services.

Several other sites such as Do Your Own Will, Rocket Lawyer, Trust & Will, and Nolo's Quicken WillMaker & Trust offer similar services. Do Your Own Will is free and the others charge fees up to $200 or require a monthly subscription. Do your research. There are many options, and many will include, for additional fees, live attorney review.

Spend Less with DIY Repairs

If you have a little bit of mechanical skill, a few tools, and an interest in saving a lot of money, think about repairing things before you replace them. DIY—do it yourself. This can range from replacing the cracked screen on a mobile phone to reviving a major appliance like a washer or dryer.

How-To Videos

Thinking about troubleshooting and disassembling a big machine can seem pretty intimidating. But you have a special resource at your fingertips that may show you how many repair jobs can be done: YouTube.

If you have any doubt about how challenging a repair might be, there's a good possibility someone somewhere has made a video showing how the job is done. The videos also provide tips and "secrets" that make some apparently impossible tasks easy. Manufacturers and parts stores make repair videos, along with thousands of individuals.

If you have an interest in automotive repairs but do not have a lift or special tools, you may be able to find a DIY automotive repair location in your area. Their services can range from simply providing tools and an empty bay where you can work to accessing lift service and providing an expert mechanic to show you exactly what to do to get the job done.

A sewing repair, fixing a crack in a trash can, patching a hole in the driveway, or replacing a window pane—YouTube has repair videos to show you how to fix nearly anything.

Acknowledgments

Work on this book began more than 15 years ago when I taught the Money Class at Integrity House in Newark, New Jersey. I met men who were incarcerated and who would face extraordinary financial challenges when they were released. In 2020, I published a book called *The Richest Man in New Babylon*. It told the story of a young man, just released from incarceration, and how he got lucky, met the right people, and learned *The Rules* for personal financial management. It is, in short, a book I wish I'd had when I first started teaching the Money Class.

In 2021, I attended a regional meeting of the Corrections Education Association (CEA) in Cape May, New Jersey. Over the course of three days, I spoke with dozens of people about *The Richest Man* and *The Rules*. After doing a workshop for conference attendees and explaining, over and over again, how *The Rules* worked, I realized that perhaps there ought to be another book. Just *The Rules*. No B.S. No Boring Stuff.

My sincere thanks to Kevin Kavanaugh, a retired corrections educator who presently serves as a director of the CEA regional executive board. Kevin opened the door to the corrections education community for me.

I am deeply indebted to Annabelle Harris, the head teacher at the North Central Correctional Institution in Gardner, Massachusetts. Annabelle saw the merit in *The Richest Man*, helped arrange a pilot class using the book, and then helped shape a curriculum for financial management in the 21st century. The work we have done on *The Richest Man* provided valuable insights and ideas that have been incorporated in this book.

Thanks to Austin Kleon. Write the book you want to read, he says, and *Keep Going*. And so, I do. And many thanks to the early readers of this book in manuscript, including Chris Riemer, David Coutinho, Ken Shapiro, and Jean Abbott. Your feedback convinced me the project had merit, and it kept me going.

Professional assistance really helps get things done. My special thanks to Pam Eidson, who served as my editor and proofreader. Pam contributed significantly to this book, adding clarity, consistency, and insight throughout the text. She spotted a thousand errors, large and small, along the way. Any that remain are entirely my own.

I must express my continued gratitude to my Foster brother, Irv.

Irvin Perry Foster passed away in September of 2021, but he lives on as Reverend Ezekiel Wright in *The Richest Man in New Babylon*. Irv was an unfailing supporter of this project and an inspiration. No matter how daunting the challenges he faced, he kept on working, supporting conflict resolution, encouraging his "kids," and trying to make the world a better place. In that, he succeeded.

Finally, as ever, my most special thanks to Jane, for her trust and support and for being, quite simply, the best person I know.

*The author on the gangplank
of H.M.S. Victory in Portsmouth, U.K.*

About the Author

Ridge Kennedy was born in Fort Smith, Arkansas. Then he moved to Philadelphia, Pennsylvania; Columbus, Ohio; Indianapolis, Indiana; Tokyo, Japan; Hatfield, Pennsylvania; Bangkok, Thailand; Fort Smith (again); Indianapolis (again); Cleveland, Ohio; and Mentor, Ohio. Then he went off to high school in New Hampshire.

No, he wasn't a military brat; his parents were in the newspaper business.

After majoring in technical theatre and set design in college, and teaching at Hiram College and Bucknell University, Ridge went into the family business, starting off as an intern at *The Evansville Press*. Over the next thirty years, he earned a living primarily as a writer: newspapers, technical writing, advertising, public relations, and marketing. In the early days of the personal computer, he expanded his interests into word processing applications and desktop publishing. In the early 2000s his career veered deeper into information technology, providing tech support, database management, and writing code instead of words.

Throughout his life, Ridge has also pursued an interest in folk music and dance. He is a song leader and dance caller. Search for "yodeling square" and his name on YouTube for a glimpse of his alter ego in the folk arts world.

His books *The Richest Man in New Babylon* and *The No B.S.* Rules for Taking Care of Your Money (*No Boring Stuff)* reflect another important area of interest for him: a deeply felt desire to make the world a better place. Not just for him, his family, and his friends, but for people he doesn't know. Fellow Americans. Fellow residents of Planet Earth. Global warming, racism, income inequality, dictators, and genocides—he worries about all that stuff, too.

His work on *The Richest Man Project* is a long-term, unfunded, altruistic effort to help address the challenges faced by people, disproportionately men of color, who have been incarcerated in the United States. But *The Rules* described in his book can be applied by anyone, anywhere, so that ticks the "income inequality" checkbox on Ridge's worry list, too.

For more information about Ridge and his ongoing projects, visit www.ridgekennedy.com. If you would like to support the effort to improve the money management skills of people who have been incarcerated, visit www.richestmaninnewbabylon.com.

Finally, if you think you will enjoy a gentle novel with music, dance, action, adventure, and romance set in the historical and literary context of Jane Austen and Regency England, be sure to read the first Dancing Master mystery: *Murder & Miss Austen's Ball*. The author is anonymous, it seems. "A Gentleman," it says on the cover. But the scribe who put pen to paper to recount this gentleman's story is one Ridgway Kennedy, a very close acquaintance of the author of this volume.

www.ingramcontent.com/pod-product-compliance
Lightning Source LLC
Chambersburg PA
CBHW061808070526
44586CB00024B/2762